£1·50

H. L. Mackenzie.

ge Ter.
felay.

A MUSIC COURSE

FOR STUDENTS

A MUSIC COURSE
FOR STUDENTS

Covering the syllabus (Ordinary Level)
of the General Certificate of Education
and similar examinations

BY

D. E. PARRY WILLIAMS

D.Mus., B.Sc., L.R.A.M.

Professor of Music at the
University College, Bangor

London
OXFORD UNIVERSITY PRESS
NEW YORK   TORONTO

Oxford University Press, Ely House, London W.1

GLASGOW NEW YORK TORONTO MELBOURNE WELLINGTON
CAPE TOWN IBADAN NAIROBI DAR ES SALAAM LUSAKA ADDIS ABABA
DELHI BOMBAY CALCUTTA MADRAS KARACHI LAHORE DACCA
KUALA LUMPUR SINGAPORE HONG KONG TOKYO

ISBN 0 19 317201 1

First Published 1937
Seventh Impression (revised) 1953
Ninth Impression (revised) 1960
Fourteenth Impression 1975

*Printed in Great Britain
by Compton Printing Ltd
London and Aylesbury*

AUTHOR'S NOTE

THIS book has been written for the use of schools, etc., where music is taught as a class subject, and the aim has been to provide, as far as possible, the subject-matter for the General Certificate and similar standards.

The sequence of chapters is not meant to indicate the actual teaching order—this being, I believe, best left to the individual teacher. The subjects have, for convenience, been treated separately, but in teaching there will naturally be a good deal of overlapping and variation in the order of treatment and presentation.

A large number of the examples to be worked have been taken from actual papers of the examining boards. I wish to express my thanks for permission to include the examples.

I am indebted for the criticism and advice which I have received from Professor David Evans and Professor Shera; and I gratefully acknowledge the help which I have received from teachers at work in the schools.

My thanks are also due to Dr. J. M. Lloyd and Dr. Joseph Morgan for their kindness in reading the proofs, and to Miss Mary Oppenheimer and Mr. D. Kighley Baxandall (formerly Assistant Keeper of Art at the National Museum of Wales), and Miss M. B. Alexander and Mr. M. E. Cooke of the University College of North Wales, Bangor, for looking through the Chronology at the end of the book.

D. E. PARRY WILLIAMS.

CONTENTS

CHAPTER I

THE RUDIMENTS OF MUSIC

1. The system of musical notation enables sounds to be represented by means of notes written on a staff, or stave.

2. A stave consists of five parallel lines with four equal spaces between them:

3. Lines and spaces are numbered upwards thus:

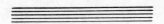

4. Notes may be written on the lines, i.e., with the lines passing through them, or in the spaces.

5. When the sign 𝄞 (Treble, or G clef) is written at the beginning of the stave, the notes assume definite names corresponding with the pitch of the sounds which they represent. The stave is then called a *Treble stave*.

E F G A B C D E F

6. Notes are named according to the first seven letters of the alphabet: A B C D E F G. The names of the lines and spaces are as follows:

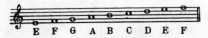

Lines
E G B D F

Spaces
F A C E

7. Middle C of the pianoforte is written on a short line (called a ' ledger-line ') below the stave.

Middle C

The note D (above Middle C) is written without a ledger-line:

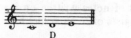

D

8. We now have the following series of notes:

9. *The Bass Clef.*
Notes belonging to a lower compass are written **with a** Bass clef:

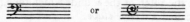

This is also called the F clef, the two dots, one on each side of the fourth line, give the position of F below Middle C.

10. The names of the notes are as follows:

2

11. *Ledger Lines*.

The use of Ledger lines enables the compass of any stave to be extended upwards, or downwards.

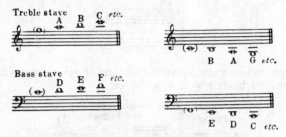

Notice that the following are identical as to pitch.

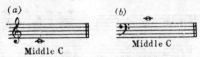

12. *Sharps and Flats*.

A *sharp* (♯) placed before a note raises its pitch one semi-tone*: a *flat* (♭) lowers it a semitone; and a *natural* (♮) restores a note previously sharpened or flattened, to its original or normal pitch.

The following, although named differently, refer to the same note on the pianoforte:

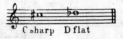

Notes which sound the same, though written differently, are said to be *enharmonic*; if the name of a note be changed without altering the pitch (as from C♯ to D♭), the *change* is said to be enharmonic.

* See p. 8, par. 1; also p. 11, par. 7.

13. Two staves may be used in combination, as in music for pianoforte or the harp; the staves are then joined together by means of a *Brace*.

Organ music is usually written on three staves, the notes on the lowest stave being played with the feet.

BACH. ' Eight Short Preludes and Fugues ', No. 1.

14. Choral music is usually written with a separate stave for each voice-part (Open score), or with only two staves (Short score), as for pianoforte.

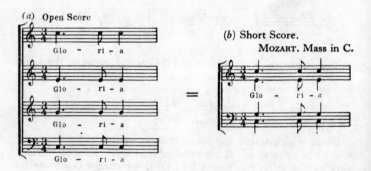

(a) Open Score

Glo — ri - a
Glo — ri - a
Glo — ri - a
Glo — ri - a

(b) Short Score.
MOZART. Mass in C.

Glo — ri - a

The Tenor part in (a) appears an octave higher than it will actually sound.

15. *Alto and Tenor Clefs*[*].

These may be used when writing for Alto and Tenor voices respectively, or for instruments of corresponding compass. They are known as *C clefs*, and indicate the position of Middle C on the stave.

An Open score for voices may now be written:

MOZART. Mass in C.

THE DURATION OF NOTES AND RESTS

1. The relative duration of sounds is indicated by means of notes of various shapes:

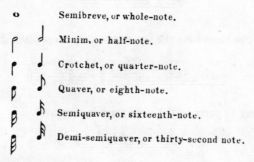

o		Semibreve, or whole-note.
	♩	Minim, or half-note.
	♩	Crotchet, or quarter-note.
	♪	Quaver, or eighth-note.
	♬	Semiquaver, or sixteenth-note.
	♬	Demi-semiquaver, or thirty-second note.

[*] Note also the *Soprano clef* found in some vocal scores:

5

Each of these notes, taken in order, has half the value of that which precedes it: taking the value of a semibreve to be four seconds, that of a minim would be two, that of a crotchet one, etc. The actual value of each note depends upon the rate at which the music is played; its relative value is constant.

Two other notes are sometimes used, viz., the *breve* , equal to two semibreves; and the *semi-demi-semiquaver* , equal to half the value of a demi-semiquaver.

2. Stems of notes are written thus: upwards to the right of the ring or dot (♩), or downwards to the left (♩).

Notes on the middle line of the stave may have their stems upwards or downwards.

Those above the middle line are written with stems downwards, those below with their stems upwards:

3. When two parts are written on the same stave, the higher part is written with all the stems upwards and the lower one with all stems downwards.

If the two parts have the same note, they are written thus:

(a) (b) (c) (d) (e)

Crossing of parts on the same stave is shown thus:

4. The duration of a note can be lengthened:

(*a*) *By writing one or more dots after it.*

A single dot lengthens a note by one-half its original value.

$$♩· = ♩ + ♪$$

A second dot adds a further quarter of its original value.

$$♩·· = ♩ + ♪ + ♬$$

(*b*) *By ' tying ' the note to another of the same pitch*.*

$$♩⌒♩ = ♩ + ♩$$

$$♩⌒♩⌒♬ = ♩ + ♩ + ♬ = ♩··$$

5. Silence in music is expressed by means of signs called '*rests*', corresponding in duration to the value of the various notes.

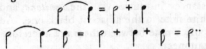

Breve.   Semibreve.   Minim.   Crotchet.

Quaver.   Semiquaver. Demi-semiquaver. Semi-demi-semiquaver.

Other *rest* signs are to be found in use; these are described on page 32, par. 4.

6. Dots after a rest indicate the same increase in duration as the corresponding dotted notes.

(*a*) 𝄼· = 𝄼 + 𝄾   (*b*) 𝄼·· = 𝄼 + 𝄾 + 𝄿

THE MAJOR SCALE

1. The white keys of a pianoforte played consecutively from C to C¹ produce a series of sounds constituting a *major scale*. It

---

* The second of two tied notes will usually be shorter than the first, excepting *possibly* from weak to strong accent.

will be felt that the note C has a particular ' home ' character: it is called the Tonic of the scale.

There are two places where a black note does not occur between adjacent white notes, viz., between E and F, and between B and C'; these sound so close together that it is impracticable to have a note between them. The distance between these notes is the smallest ' working distance ' in music, viz., the *semitone*, and is the same as from a white note to the adjacent black one. Adjacent white notes with a black note between them are therefore a *tone* apart (i.e., two semitones).

2. A *major scale* is an alphabetical succession of sounds consisting of tones and semitones—the latter occurring between the 3rd and 4th, and 7th and 8th degrees of the scale.

The degrees of the scale have the following names:

First degree	TONIC	Keynote.
Second ,,	SUPERTONIC	The note *above* the Tonic.
Third ,,	MEDIANT	The note midway between Tonic and Dominant.
Fourth ,,	SUBDOMINANT	The ' lower ' Dominant: occupies a position *below* the Tonic corresponding to that of the Dominant *above* it.
Fifth ,,	DOMINANT	Next in importance to the Tonic.
Sixth ,,	SUBMEDIANT	The ' lower ' Mediant: the note midway between the Tonic and the ' lower ' Dominant.
Seventh ,,	LEADING NOTE	The note that *leads* to the Tonic.

8

3. A major scale can be divided into two similar halves called *tetrachords*, each containing two tones and one semitone.

4. *Scale formation.*

The major scale can be reproduced at any pitch.

(*a*) *Scale of G major.* Take the *upper* tetrachord of C major, and add an *equal* tetrachord commencing a tone above it.

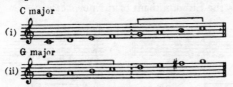

The use of F♯ becomes necessary in (ii) in order that the position of the semitone shall be exactly the same in both tetrachords.

(*b*) *Scale of F major.* Take the *lower* tetrachord of C major, and add an *equal* tetrachord below it.

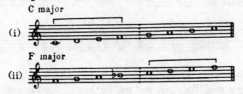

5. *A series of major scales* can now be formed, each succeeding scale commencing on the Dominant or 5th degree of the preceding scale, and having one *sharp* more; the extra sharp produces the Leading note of the new scale.

9

A corresponding series of major scales can be formed similarly, each succeeding scale commencing on the *Subdominant*, or 4th degree of the preceding scale, and having *one flat* more; the extra flat produces the Subdominant of the new scale.

6. *Key-signature*.

The sharps and flats proper to the key of a composition are written together at the beginning of each stave, and immediately after the clef; they constitute the key-signature*.

* Ledger lines are never used for a key-signature.

Sharps are written commencing with F♯, each succeeding sharp being placed slightly to the right of the preceding one, and on the fourth step below or the fifth above.

Flats commence with B♭; each succeeding flat is written slightly to the right, and on the fourth step above or the fifth below*.

7. A sharp, flat or natural may be used as an *accidental* to sharpen or flatten temporarily any note of the scale†. An accidental takes effect only at the pitch at which it is written and does not affect the note an octave above or below.

(a)   (b)

8. Unless contradicted, an accidental continues to affect succeeding notes of the same pitch for the remainder of the bar, and also for the *first* note in the next, if tied as in (b):

(a)   (b)

Otherwise, the accidental should be rewritten:

SCHUBERT. Symphony in C.

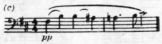

In the following, it is safer to use the ♮ as a *cautionary* sign, although strictly speaking it is unnecessary.

WAGNER. ' Tristan und Isolde.'

(c)

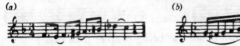

* The keynote of a major scale (sharp keys) will therefore be one step above the sharp farthest to the right. In the case of a flat signature, the flat farthest to the right gives the Subdominant of the scale; with more than one flat, the penultimate flat gives the Tonic.

† The note is then *chromatic*.

9. *Double-sharps and Double-flats.*

A note already sharpened may be raised a semitone further; the sign is × placed before the note.

A note already flattened may similarly be lowered a semitone; the sign is ♭♭.

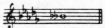

Two ways have been used to contradict a double-sharp or flat:

Method (*b*) is recommended as being simpler than (*a*).

10. The following is an arrangement of keys in order of their closest relationship; each key-note is the Dominant or the Sub-dominant of its neighbour.

TABLE OF KEYS

THE MINOR SCALE

1. The minor scale derives its origin from the Aeolian mode*.

2. Two forms of the scale have emerged :

(a) The Melodic Minor Scale—produced by raising a semitone the 6th and 7th degrees of the mode ascending, and restoring them coming down.

A minor
Ascending   Descending

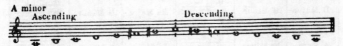

(b) The Harmonic Minor Scale—produced by raising the 7th degree of the mode only, ascending and descending.

A minor (Harmonic form)

Note the unvocal interval between the 6th and 7th degrees of the scale.

3. *Key-signature of a minor scale*—RELATIVE MINOR.

The key-signature of A minor represents the *descending Melodic form*, and is therefore the same as that of C major. The two scales are said to be *related*, and A minor is called the relative minor of C major: it begins a Minor 3rd (three semitones) lower than the major scale.

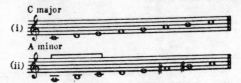

* *Modes:* The forerunners of our modern major and minor scales, each mode corresponding to the *white* notes of the piano played consecutively from a note to its octave, thus: D to D¹ = Dorian Mode; A to A¹ = Aeolian Mode, etc.

SHARP KEYS			FLAT KEYS		
Major Key	Rel. Minor		Major Key	Rel. Minor	
C Major	A Minor		C Major	A Minor	
G Major	E Minor		F Major	D Minor	
D Major	B Minor		B♭ Major	G Minor	
A Major	F♯ Minor		E♭ Major	C Minor	
E Major	C♯ Minor		A♭ Major	F Minor	
B Major	G♯ Minor		D♭ Major	B♭ Minor	
F♯ Major	D♯ Minor		G♭ Major	E♭ Minor	
C♯ Major	A♯ Minor		C♭ Major	A♭ Minor	

5. Writing a Minor scale.

To write the scale of E minor (Melodic and Harmonic forms).

Take the series of eight notes E–E' as found in the scale of G, the relative major of E minor.

For the Melodic form of the scale.

Raise the 6th and 7th degrees a semitone each, ascending; and restore them coming down.*

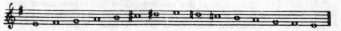

* For other scales, e.g., *C minor*, other *accidentals* must be used. See pp. 11 and 12, par. 7 and 9.

For the Harmonic form.

Raise the 7th degree only, ascending and descending.

6. *Tonic Major and Tonic Minor*.

When a major and minor scale both have the same key-note one is said to be the Tonic major or the Tonic minor of the other; thus C major is the Tonic major of C minor, C minor the Tonic minor of C major.

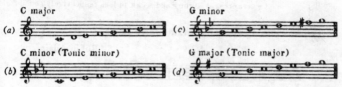

It will be noticed that a Tonic minor scale has three flats more (or three sharps less) than its Tonic major.

If x be the number of sharps in the key-signature of a major scale, the number contained in the signature of the Tonic minor is $x-3$ sharps, or $x+3$ flats, a (–) *sharp* being regarded as a flat.

ACCENT AND TIME. BARS.

1. Some notes in a melody are more strongly accented than others; it will be found that the strongest accents occur regularly.

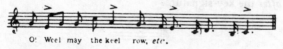

O! Weel may the keel row, *etc.*

2. Bar-lines are used to indicate the regularly recurring accent: they are drawn vertically across the stave, immediately before the strong accent.

O! Weel may the keel row, *etc.*

The distance from one bar-line to the next is called a *measure* or (more commonly) *a bar*.

3. A bar may be divided into equal pulses or beats; the arrangement of the beats (in groups of two or three, etc.) constitutes the *Time* of the music.

Duple Time. Each bar contains *two* beats.

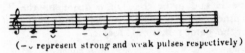

HAYDN. ' Surprise ' Symphony

(— ⌣ represent strong and weak pulses respectively)

Triple Time. Each bar contains *three* beats.

' Robin Adair.'

Quadruple Time.

' St Anne.'

(V represents a medium accent)

4. A beat may have the duration of a minim, crotchet, quaver, etc. It is usual to indicate the *number* of the beats in each bar, and also the *value* of each beat: this is shown by means of a TIME-SIGNATURE written at the commencement of the music, immediately *after* the key-signature.

The upper figure 2 indicates the number of beats to a bar, the lower figure 4 signifies that the value of each beat is a crotchet, i.e., one-fourth of a semibreve.

If the time of the music changes, a new signature must be used *.

*A persistent fluctuation of times may, however, be indicated by means of a dual time-signature: *vide* p. 63, ex. (b).

16

5. *Simple and Compound Time.* Subdivision of Pulses.

(a) *Simple Time.*

When the actual, or implied, subdivision of the beats is into halves, the time is said to be *Simple*.

Exceptionally, in Simple time, a beat or beats may be sub-divided into thirds: such subdivisions are called *Triplets*, and are indicated by a figure 3 written above the triplet group.

(b) *Compound Time.*

When the subdivision of the beats into thirds becomes a con-sistent feature of the music, the time is said to be *Compound*. The beats are then represented by dotted notes.

The time-signature in this case will show the possible number of triplet divisions in each bar, and the value of each note in a triplet.

The triplet figure <u>3</u> is not used in Compound time, since each *dotted* note (representing the beat) is itself divisible into three.

6. *Table illustrating Simple and Compound Time.*

Simple Duple. Compound Duple.

Simple Triple.   *Compound Triple.*

Simple Quadruple.   *Compound Quadruple.*

7. Note the difference between the following:

8. *Common Time; Alla breve.*

⁴⁄₄ time is usually called Common time: it is indicated by a C thus*:

Alla breve is the old name for ⁴⁄₂ time, but it is **frequently** misused to mean two beats to a bar.

The sign 𝄵 indicates ²⁄₂ time: it is often wrongly used instead of ⁴⁄₂.

9. ⁵⁄₄ *and* ⁷⁄₄ *Time.*

In ⁵⁄₄ the beats may be grouped 2+3 or 3+2.

TSCHAIKOWSKY. Symphony No. VI.   HOLST. 'The Perfect Fool.'

* The sign C has nothing to do with the C of Common, but is a modernized form of the semicircle, used in medieval music as a symbol for *tempus imperfectus* or the division of the breve (or unit) into two semibreves. '*Perfect*' time was shown by means of a *complete* circle, and implied a subdivision of the unit into three semibreves.

In $\frac{7}{4}$ the grouping is usually 3+4 or 4+3.

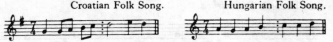
Croatian Folk Song.   Hungarian Folk Song.

INTERVALS

1. *An interval is the difference in pitch between two sounds.*

2. The following, being found in the Major scale, serve as a standard by which other intervals may be estimated.

Major 2nd   Major 3rd   Perfect 4th   Perfect 5th
(2 Semitones) (4 Semitones) (5 Semitones) (7 Semitones)

Major 6th   Major 7th   Perfect 8th or Octave
(9 Semitones) (11 Semitones) (12 Semitones)

They are named according to the number of letter-names in their formation: C–E includes the letters C, D, E, and is described as a *Third*.

3. The intervals of the Major Diatonic scale are classified thus:
   Perfect intervals. 4th, 5th and the Octave (above the Tonic).
   Major intervals. 2nd, 3rd, 6th and the 7th (above the Tonic).

4. Either of the notes forming an interval may be inflected, i.e., sharpened or flattened. Inflection of a note does not alter the numerical description of an interval, but it changes its quality.

(*a*) *Major* intervals become *Minor* when decreased a semitone.

Min. 2nd   Min. 2nd   Min. 3rd   Min. 6th   Min. 7th

(*b*) *Minor thirds and sevenths* may be further flattened a semitone and become *Diminished*.

Dim. 3rd   Dim. 3rd   Dim. 3rd

Dim. 7th   Dim. 7th   Dim. 7th

19

(c) *Perfect* intervals may be decreased by one semitone only: they become *Diminished*.

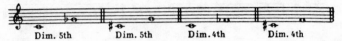

Dim. 5th   Dim. 5th   Dim. 4th   Dim. 4th

(d) Major seconds and sixths and all Perfect intervals can be increased a semitone: they become *Augmented*.

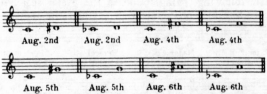

Aug. 2nd   Aug. 2nd   Aug. 4th   Aug. 4th

Aug. 5th   Aug. 5th   Aug. 6th   Aug. 6th

Note.—An Augmented 4th is called a *tritone*, i.e., three tones. *There are no Augmented 3rds or 7ths, Diminished 2nds or 6ths**.

5. An interval of any particular denomination, e.g., 2nd, 3rd, 4th, etc., occurs only in three forms.

2nd	3rd	4th	5th	6th	7th
Augmented	——	Augmented	Augmented	Augmented	——
——	——	Perfect	Perfect	——	——
Major	Major	——	——	Major	Major
Minor	Minor	——	——	Minor	Minor
——	Diminished	Diminished	Diminished	——	Diminished

6. *Consonant and Dissonant intervals.*

Major and Minor 3rds and 6ths and Perfect intervals (excepting the 4th) are said to be *Consonant* intervals: they do not require to be followed by another interval in order to make their effect satisfactory.

The Perfect 4th, 2nds, 7ths, 9ths and all Augmented and Diminished intervals are said to be *Dissonant*: they require to be resolved into a Consonance in order to make their effect satisfactory.

7. *The Unison.*

Two voices producing the same sound (i.e., identical as to pitch) are said to be *in unison*.

* I.e., they are not found in the Chromatic Scale.

The Unison is not strictly an interval, and therefore cannot be augmented or diminished; the following should be described as a *Chromatic semitone**.

8. Intervals greater than an octave are called *Compound intervals*.

Major 9th   Major 10th   Perfect 5th
             or 3rd   or 12th

Excepting the Major 9th, it is usual to name a Compound interval by the Simple interval which it contains, the numerical value of the Compound interval being that of the Simple interval plus 7—a Major 10th equals a Major $(3+7)$.

9. *Inverting an interval.*

An interval may be inverted by placing the lower note an octave higher, or the upper note an octave lower.

(a) Major 3rd   Inversion
                   Min. 6th

(b) Major 3rd   Inversion
                   Min. 6th

NOTE.—*Major* intervals when inverted become *Minor*.
     Minor intervals become *Major*.
     Diminished intervals become *Augmented*.
     Augmented intervals become *Diminished*.
     Perfect intervals remain *Perfect*.

The numerical value of an inverted interval is $(9 - x)$ where x is the numerical value of the original interval. A Major 3rd becomes a Minor 6th, i.e. $(9 - 3)$.

---

* *Chromatic semitone*. Strictly speaking, a Chromatic semitone signifies a semitone higher or lower than a natural note of a scale. It is frequently, however, used for the distance between two notes a semitone apart, having the *same* letter-name (C–C♯; D–D♭, etc.).

A *Diatonic* semitone is the distance between two notes a semitone apart, and having *different* letter-names (E–F; B–C, etc.).

10. *Naming intervals.*

Ex. *To name the interval:*

Regard the lower note (G) as a temporary Tonic of a Major scale.

The note D is now found to be the 5th degree of the scale, and the interval G–D is therefore a *Perfect 5th.*

Ex. *To name the interval:*

Regarding the lower note as a temporary Tonic we get the scale of D major.

This contains the interval D–C♯ (the Major 7th from D), whereas the given interval is from D–C♮, i.e., one semitone less, or a *Minor 7th.*

Ex. *To name the interval:*

Invert the given interval: this gives A–E♯, i.e., an Augmented 5th. By inverting back and calculating the name of the inversion, we obtain the name of the given interval, viz., *a Diminished 4th.*

11. *Writing a note at the required interval from a given note.*

Ex. *To write an Augmented 6th above E♭.*

Regard the given note as a temporary Tonic: the *Major* 6th from E♭ is C, and the required note is C♯, i.e., one semitone higher.

Ex. *To write a Diminished 7th below D.*

The inversion of the Diminished 7th gives an Augmented 2nd. Write an Augmented 2nd above the given note (D) and invert the interval:

Aug. 2nd   Dim. 7th

12. *Naming the keys in which a given interval occurs.*

Ex. *Name the keys in which the interval* [♯ notation] *occurs.*

(a) Name the given interval: a Major 3rd.

(b) Write the scales of C major and C minor (Harmonic form), adding *diatonic* thirds* above each degree of each scale.

C major

C minor

A Major 3rd can occur on the 1st, 4th, and 5th degrees of a major scale; and on the 3rd, 5th, and 6th degrees of a minor scale.

The interval G–B can therefore occur on (i) the 1st degree of G major, (ii) the 4th degree of D major, (iii) the 5th degree of C major and minor, (iv) the 6th degree of B minor, and (v) the 3rd degree of E minor.

(i) G major   (ii) D major

(iii) C major and minor   (iv) B minor

(v)

* Diatonic thirds, i.e., produced from the ordinary notes of the scale.

The above method can be used similarly for other common intervals. The keys in which Augmented and Diminished intervals occur are found as follows:

Augmented 2nd, 4th and 5th, and their inversions.

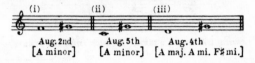

Aug. 2nd [A minor]   Aug. 5th [A minor]   Aug. 4th [A maj. A mi. F♯ mi.]

In (i) and (ii) the upper note is the Leading-note of the *minor* scale in which the interval occurs.

In (iii) the upper note is the Leading-note of the *major* scale in which the interval occurs, and also of its *Tonic* minor; it is also the Supertonic of the *Relative* minor.

In the inversion of the above intervals, the *lower* note is the Leading-note of the scale.

The occurrence of one of these intervals between *any* two notes in a passage will enable the key to be determined. Such notes must, of course, be diatonic. See p. 25 re *Finding the key of a given passage.*

The Augmented 6th.

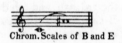

Chrom. Scales of B and E

The lower note of the interval (or the upper note of its inversion) gives the Minor 2nd or the Minor 6th of the Chromatic scale (*vide* p. 27) in which the interval occurs.

Ex. *Name the keys in which the following interval occurs:*

The interval is a *Diminished 5th*: its lower note is therefore the 7th degree of the *major* scale in which the interval occurs, i.e., F♯ major. It is also found in the Tonic minor and Relative minor of that scale, i.e., F♯ minor and D♯ minor.

FINDING THE KEY OF A GIVEN PASSAGE

NOTE.—*It is not always possible to do this without a knowledge of the* harmony *of the passage: this should always be studied where possible.*

1. Observe whether the passage contains two notes (not necessarily consecutive) which make a characteristic interval, viz., a Diminished 4th, 5th or 7th, or the inversion of one of these. Find the key, or keys, in which this interval can occur by the method described on the previous page.

HAYDN. Quartet in C, Op. 1, No. 6.

The interval from Bb (bar 2) to E♮ (bar 3) is a Diminished 5th and it can occur in F major, F minor, and D minor. The context must now decide.

C♯ (bar 4) rules out both F major and F minor and therefore fixes the key as *D minor**.

2. *The ' sharpest note ' in the passage is the Leading note of the scale.*

Take each note in turn and imagine it as the Leading note of a scale. That which leads to the key with most sharps (or fewest flats) is the ' sharpest note '.

Ex. *To find the key of the following passage:*

(i)   BEETHOVEN. Quartet in C major.

Arrange the notes in order of sharpness: . . . B, C♯, G♯.

This gives G♯ as the ' sharpest ' note, i.e., the Leading note of the scale. The Tonic is therefore A, and the key is A major or minor.   The presence of C♯ (the *Major* 3rd above A) indicates *A major.*

(ii)   BRAHMS. Quintet in F.

* Or taking the Diminished 7th between Bb and C♯, this can occur only in *one* key: *D minor.*

Here the ' sharpest ' note is A♮ and the key-note is B♭. The passage contains the *Minor* 3rd from B♭, and the key is therefore B♭ minor.

3. *Chromatic notes.*

The context must decide whether a note is *diatonic* or *chromatic*. In the following passage the F♯ is clearly a chromatic note, and will not be taken into consideration when finding the ' sharpest ' note.

MOZART. ' Jupiter ' Symphony.

The key of the passage is C major, the *sharpest note* being B♮.

TRANSPOSITION

A knowledge of intervals enables a given passage to be *transposed*, i.e., written at a higher or lower pitch, as required.

Ex. *To transpose the following passage a Minor 3rd higher:*

LALO. ' Le Roi d'Ys.'

(*a*) *Find the key of the passage.* The signature indicates F major, or D minor; the notes C♯ and F (together) suggest D minor.

(*b*) *Fix the Tonic of the new key and write the key-signature.* This will be a Minor 3rd above D, and the passage must be re-written in the key of F minor; the new key-signature is:

(*c*) Transpose the passage a Minor 3rd higher, reproducing the *melodic* intervals as from C, thus:

A to F in the original passage=a Minor 6th.
F to E=a Diatonic semitone.
E to D=a Major 2nd, etc.

NOTE.—If two consecutive notes have *different* letter-names in the original, these must also be different when transposed. The following transposition would obviously be wrong:

(a)   (b) Incorrectly transposed

THE CHROMATIC SCALE

1. A Chromatic scale is one which proceeds entirely by semi-tones from a note to its octave.

2. It is written in three forms:
   (a) The Harmonic Chromatic scale.
   (b) The Melodic Chromatic scale of a *major* key.
   (c) The Melodic Chromatic scale of a *minor* key.

3. *To write the Harmonic Chromatic scale of C.*
This has the same form ascending and descending.

(i) Write a major scale commencing with C, with each note twice, except the Tonic and Dominant.

(ii) Fill in with accidentals so as to produce a semitone between each note; sharpen the Subdominant and flatten the 2nd and 3rd, and 6th and 7th degrees of the major scale; the Tonic and Dominant remain unchanged.

Harmonic Chromatic scale of C.

The same scale may also be written as follows:
(a) Begin with the major scale of C, spaced thus:

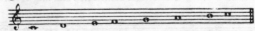

(b) Add notes from the *Tonic minor scale* (both forms, ascending and descending) which do not occur in the above:

From Harm. Min.   From Melodic Min.

(c) Complete by adding the *Chromatic* semitone* above F (the Subdominant) and the *Diatonic* semitone above the key-note.

Harmonic Chromatic scale of C.

It will be noticed that the letter-names of the Tonic and Dominant are the only ones which do not occur twice in succession: the Subdominant is always sharpened.

4. *The Melodic Chromatic scale.* The Arbitrary Chromatic scale.
This has two forms, viz., ascending and descending. The descending form has the same notation as the Harmonic Chromatic scale.

(a) *For a major key.*
Write a major scale with the *Mediant and Leading note once*, and all other notes *twice*.

Add accidentals making Chromatic semitones as from C.
Melodic Chromatic scale of C (ascending form).

Descending form (same as Harmonic Chromatic scale).

(b) *For a minor key.*
Commence with the Harmonic Minor scale of C and add the Minor 7th; fill in with Chromatic semitones starting from C.

The descending form is the same as the Harmonic Chromatic scale.

* See p. 21, footnote.

28

5. Chromatic scales. General considerations.

(i) Neither the Tonic nor the Dominant is ever flattened.

(ii) No letter-name occurs more than twice in succession.

(iii) The Subdominant of the diatonic scale is always sharpened.

6. Other scales in use.

Two other scales are freely used, viz., the *Pentatonic* and the *Whole-tone scale*.

The *Pentatonic scale* consists of five notes, and may be regarded for practical purposes as an ordinary major scale with its 4th and 7th degrees omitted.

The octave being reached on the sixth note, it will be obvious that some of the notes must be more than a tone apart.

The notes of the Pentatonic scale correspond with the black notes of the piano played consecutively from G♭ to its octave.

The *Whole-tone scale* consists of equal steps of a Major 2nd and is usually written commencing with C♮ or D♭.

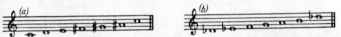

No *perfect* intervals occur in the scale—the fifths are all augmented and the thirds all major. The scale was used extensively by Debussy.

THE GROUPING OF NOTES

1. For convenience in reading, notes shorter than crotchets should be grouped together so that the natural divisions of the bar (i.e., the beats) *are clearly represented to the eye.*

PURCELL.

Here the notes belonging to the same beat are grouped together; a group should not normally extend beyond one beat.

29

2. Exceptions to the rule are found as follows:

(i) In ⁴⁄₄ time, four quavers may be grouped together in the first half of the bar or the second:

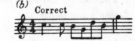

The principle to be observed is: *that the halves of the bars should be clearly indicated by the grouping:*

(ii) In ³⁄₄, ³⁄₈, ³⁄₁₆ time the six quavers, semiquavers, etc., may be grouped together thus:

BEETHOVEN.   MOZART.

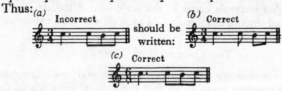

3. Care should be taken to make the distinction between *Simple Triple* and *Compound Duple time* quite clear.
Thus:

should be written:

4. Two or more notes sung to a single syllable (in vocal music) are grouped together thus:

PURCELL

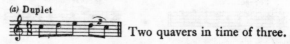

Mus - es   bring   your   ro - ses   hi - ther.

5. *Unusual grouping of notes:*

(a) Duplet

Two quavers in time of three.

30

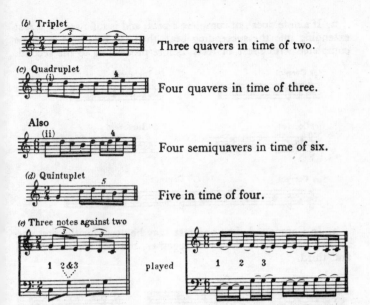

(b) Triplet — Three quavers in time of two.

(c) Quadruplet (i) — Four quavers in time of three.

Also (ii) — Four semiquavers in time of six.

(d) Quintuplet — Five in time of four.

(e) Three notes against two ... played

The note G in the bass comes immediately *after* the second note of the triplet group.

THE GROUPING OF RESTS

1. Generally speaking, rests of greater value than a beat should not be used.

(a) Correct   *(b)* Incorrect   *(c)* Correct   *(d)* Incorrect

(e) Correct   *(f)* Incorrect

Except to indicate a clear half-bar at the beginning or end of a bar in 4/4 time.

(g) Correct   *(h)* Incorrect   *(i)* Correct

2. If a note does not complete a beat, and is followed by a rest extending into the succeeding beat, then the first beat must be completed with a rest, or rests, before proceeding to the second.

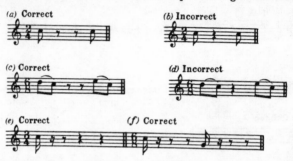

3. In Compound time one rest may be used for the first and second divisions of the beats together, but not for the second and third.

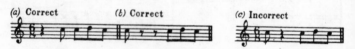

4. A whole bar's rest is always indicated by means of a Semibreve rest, irrespective of the Time in which the music is written*.

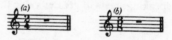

A rest of more than one bar is written thus:

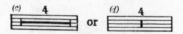

The number above the dash indicates the number of bars rest.

---

* Except in true *Alla breve* ($\frac{4}{2}$) time, when a Breve rest is written instead.

SYNCOPATION

Syncopation is a displacement or disturbance of the normal accent.

It may be produced in the following ways:

(i) By beginning a note on a normally weak beat, or part of a beat, and prolonging it into the next.

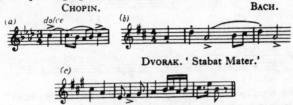

CHOPIN.   BACH.

DVORAK. ' Stabat Mater.'

(ii) By means of dynamic emphasis.

HAYDN. Pianoforte Sonata.

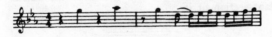

(iii) By using a rest on a normally strong beat.

CHOPIN.

BARRING A GIVEN PASSAGE

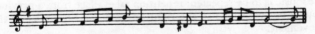

1. Examine the passage for characteristic groups indicating Simple or Compound time.

♩ ♫ suggests ⁶⁄₈ time (Compound), but is often written instead of : ♩. ♪ ♫

♪ ♩ ♩ ♪ suggests Syncopation, and may represent ³⁄₄ or ⁶⁄₈ time.

♩. ♫ ♫ points towards Simple ³⁄₄ time.

2. Examine the *end* of the passage. If the last note is a long one, the passage probably commences on the first beat of the bar: the last bar need not be a complete bar, but the notes at the beginning, when added to it, should complete the value of a bar.

Now try to bar the given passage:

The time is clearly $\frac{3}{4}$ or $\frac{6}{8}$. In bar 1 it might be either*, and similarly in bar 2, but in bars 3 and 4 it cannot be $\frac{6}{8}$ as the grouping of the notes makes this impossible. It must therefore be $\frac{3}{4}$.

SIGNS AND ABBREVIATIONS

1. A double-bar indicates the end of a movement, or an important section of it.

2. A double-bar preceded by two or four dots signifies that the music is to be repeated: repetition takes place from a previous double-bar with dots to the right or from the beginning of the movement.

3. Variation of the termination of a passage on repetition is shown thus:

---

* Since it may be a measure of $\frac{3}{4}$ incorrectly written, as is frequently the case.

34

On repetition the 2nd-time bar is to be played instead of the preceding one.

4. The letters D.C. (Da Capo) and D.$. (Dal Segno) are also used to indicate a *repeat*.

D.C. means repeat from the beginning and continue to the word *Fine**.

D.$. means repeat from the point marked with the sign 𝄋 and continue to the word *Fine*.

Bis is sometimes used to indicate that a bar or small section of the music is to be played *twice*.

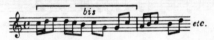

5. *A pause,* ⌢ written over or under a note or rest means that the note or rest is to be prolonged at the discretion of the performer. If a considerable pause is intended, the words *Lunga Pausa* are used.

The letters G.P. are used in orchestral music to signify silence for the whole orchestra.

6. *8va*, with or without a dotted line, means that a passage is to be played an octave higher than written. Resumption of ordinary pitch is indicated by the cessation of the dotted line or by the word *loco*.

* Or to a 'hold' ⌢, sometimes used instead of the word *Fine*.

8va bassa, or *8va sotto*, written under the notes of the bass stave, signifies that they are to be played an octave lower.

8ves (Con 8, or 8) means that a passage is to be played in octaves.

7. A *slur*, ⌒ or ⌣, written above or below two or more consecutive notes indicates that they are to be played in a smooth, connected manner, with an almost imperceptible shortening of the last note. It is also used:

(*a*) *To mark the phrasing.*

BEETHOVEN. Pianoforte Sonata.

(*b*) *To indicate notes sung to a single syllable in vocal music.*

BACH. B minor Mass.

Glo — — ri - a in - ex - cel (-sis)

(*c*) (i) *To indicate the bowing of a string passage.* Notes written with a slur are to be played with one bow, i.e., one *stroke* of a bow.

HANDEL. Violin Sonata in A.

(ii) To show (for a keyed or wind instrument) that the notes are to be played without perceptible break between them.

BRUCKNER. Symphony VII.

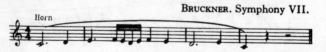

Horn

8. Notes played in a short detached manner produce the effect of *Staccato*. The three grades of staccato are:

(*a*) Staccato

SCHUMANN. Fughetta.

(*b*) Staccatissimo

BRAHMS. Piano Sonata.

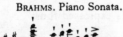

As short and as detached as possible.

(*c*) Mezzo Staccato

BRAHMS. String Sextet.

Half Staccato, with slight stress on the marked notes *vide* par. 9.

9. The sign – under or over a note indicates slightly more than the normal stress.

MAHLER. Symphony No. IV in G.

10. *Sforzando* (*sf* or *fz*).

Emphasis upon a particular note is shown by means of a sign > or ʌ written above it. A short, forceful accent upon a given note is called sforzando and is indicated by the letters *sf* or *fz* above it.

11. *Reiterated notes*.

(i) A note written with one or more strokes above it is to be reiterated instead of being held. The *number* of strokes signifies the frequency of reiteration—one stroke representing quavers, two strokes semiquavers, etc.; the *value* of the written note represents the duration of reiteration.

(ii) Rapid alternation of *two* notes is expressed thus:

The *duration* of the alternation is expressed by the written note, the *speed* by the number of strokes. Note that the total value of the semiquavers in each example equals *one* only of the written notes.

12. *Tremolando.*

Notes to be alternated or reiterated as quickly as possible are written thus:

13. *Signs for repeated groups of notes:*

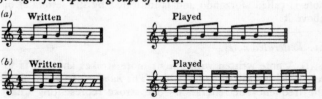

One stroke signifies repetition of the preceding group of quavers, *two* strokes represent a group of semiquavers.

Repetition of the previous bar, or part of a bar, is indicated thus:

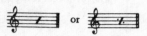

14. *Arpeggio.*

In an arpeggio the notes of a chord are played in rapid succession upwards or downwards, each note, when sounded, being held for the remaining duration of the written note. The sign is a vertical undulating line ($\oint$) placed before the written notes of the chord.

There are three forms of arpeggio in common use:

The downward arpeggio sign $\{$ is now obsolete.

ORNAMENTS

Composers who wrote for harpsichord and other early keyed instruments (except the organ) had two main difficulties to face, viz.: that the notes, as played, could neither be sustained nor appreciably accented. These peculiarities or defects were overcome by the use of Ornaments, i.e., skilful decorations around a note, which gave to it a semblance of duration and of accent. The following are the ornaments in common use.

	Moderate Tempo	Quick Tempo

Appoggiatura

Duration of Appoggiatura equals half that of the written (principal) note: it is played *on* the accent.

The Appoggiatura here takes two-thirds the value of the dotted note.

Acciaccatura

Played as quickly as possible *on* the accent which the *principal* note retains.

Mordent
(a) Upper Mordent (b) Lower Mordent

A single short alternation of a principal note with the note above (or below) followed by the principal note accented.

Extended Mordent

Trill or Shake

Rapid alternation of principle note with the note above it, ending, generally, with a *turn* on the principal note. (see also footnote).

Turn **Inverted T.***

Inverted T.

Turn *after* a Note

Turn after a *dotted* **Note**

Hold principal note for the greater part of its value before commencing the turn.

In Compound-time

The last note of the turn† takes the value of the dot.

* Also indicated by ∽ or ♁.

NOTE: In *Bach* and *Handel*, commence a trill with the note *above* the principal except:

    (a) at the beginning of a phrase, or after a rest, or staccato note;

    (b) when the trill occurs on the second note of a characteristic interval;

    (c) following a note of higher pitch.

TERMS USED IN MUSIC

RELATING TO PACE.

Adagio—Leisurely but not so slow as *Largo.*

Allegro—Quick, lively.

Allegretto—Less quickly than *Allegro.*

Andante—Going easily at a moderate pace.

Andantino—Strictly a somewhat *slower* rate than *Andante* but used generally to signify a pace somewhat faster than *Andante.*

Grave—Very slow, solemn.

Largamente—In a broad style: similar in meaning to *Largo.*

Largo—Broad, stately, and very slow.

Larghetto—Slow, but not so slow as *Largo.*

Lento—Slower than *Andante*, but not so slow as *Largo.*

Moderato—At a moderate pace.

Presto—Quicker than *Allegro.*

Prestissimo—Very quickly.

Tempo comodo—At an easy, convenient pace.

Tempo ordinario—At a moderate pace.

Vivo, Vivace—Lively, briskly.

Met.—An indication of speed as shown by the *Metronome.* Met. 60, or M.M.=60, represents sixty pulses (beats) a minute. M.M.=*Maelzel's Metronome.*

MODIFICATION OF PACE.

Accelerando (accel.)—Getting gradually quicker.

Ad libitum, A piacere—The manner of performance (pace, etc.) being left to the discretion of the performer.

Allargando—Decreasing in speed, broadening.

A tempo, Tempo—Returning to normal time.

Calando—Gradually decreasing in pace and tone.

Doppio movimento—*Double* the pace.

L'istesso tempo—Used sometimes with a change of time-signature, e.g. $\frac{2}{2}-\frac{2}{4}$, to indicate that the value of each *beat* remains the same in the new time as in the old.

Mancando—Similar in meaning to *Calando* (*q.v.*), also *Morendo*, *Perdendosi* and *Smorzando*.

Meno allegro—Less quickly.

Meno mosso—With less movement; slackening in pace.

Perdendosi—see *Calando*.

Più mosso—With more movement; quickening.

Ritardando (*ritard.*) ⎫
Rallentando (*rall.*) ⎬ Getting gradually slower.
Ritenuto (*rit.*) ⎭

Stretto ⎫
Stringendo ⎬ Increasing the pace.

Tempo primo—Returning to the original pace.

Tempo giusto—In exact time.

Tempo rubato—Allowing the performer freedom to lengthen and shorten notes (more or less imperceptibly) with a view to securing elasticity of line or of phrase, literally 'robbed time'.

Terms Relating to Manner of Performance.

A—In, according to. *A cappella*—in a church style.

Affettuoso—Tenderly, with feeling.

Agitato—Agitated, restless.

Amabile—Tenderly, gently.

Amoroso—In a gentle style (literally 'lovingly ').

Animato—With spirit, or with animation.

Appassionato, -a; Con passione—Impassioned, with deep feeling.

Assai—Very.

Attacca—Proceed immediately.

Ben—Well. *Ben marcato*—Well marked.

Brillante—Brilliantly.

Cantabile, Cantando—In a singing style.

Col or *Colla*—With the . . .

Colla voce—Following the solo part closely.

Con—With. *Con brio*—With vigour.

Con forza—With force.

Con fuoco—With fire.

42

Con grazia—Gracefully, elegantly.
Con moto—With movement.

Da capo al fine—(Repeat) from the beginning, and end at the word ' *Fine* '.
Dal segno (D.$)—Return to the sign.
Dolce—Sweetly.
Dolente, Doloroso—Sadly, plaintively.

E or *Ed.*—And.
Espressivo—With expression.

Fuoco—Fire.
Furioso—Impetuously, wildly.

Giocoso, Giocosamente—Playfully, jocosely.
Grazioso—Gracefully.

Il or *La*—The.

Legato—Smoothly.
Leggiero, Leggieramente—Lightly.
Lusingando—Soothingly.

Ma—But.
Maestoso—With dignity, majestically.
Meno—Less.
Mesto—Sadly.
Mezzo—Half, e.g., *Mezzo forte*—moderately loud.
Molto—Very. *Di molto*—Extremely.
Mosso—Moved. Cf. *Meno* — and *Più* —.
Movimento—Speed. *Doppio movimento*—Twice as fast.

Non—Not. *Non tanto*—Not so much. *Non troppo*—Not too much.

Parlando, Parlante—As if speaking.
Pesante—Heavily.
Piacevole—Pleasantly, smoothly.
Piangevole—Sadly, plaintively.
Più—More.
Poco—Little, slightly. *Poco a poco*—Little by little.
Poi—Then.
Poi La Coda—Means : *Then to the Coda.*
Pomposo—Pompously, majestically.
Portamento—(Used in singing); the voice to be carried with extreme smoothness from one note to the other.

Quasi—As if, almost.

Risoluto—Determined, resolutely.

Scherzando, Scherzoso—Playfully, piquantly, humorously.
Sempre—Always, throughout the movement or section.
Senza—Without.
Soave, Suave—Sweetly, flowingly.
Sostenuto—Sustained.
Sotto voce—In an undertone.
Staccato—Short, detached.
Strepitoso—Loudly, boisterously.

Tacet—Indicates that the part so marked has nothing to play during the whole movement or passage.
Tanto—So much. *Allegro non tanto*—Not so fast.
Tenuta, Tenuto, Tenute, Ten.—Held on, sustained.
Tranquillo, Tranquillamente—Quietly, calmly.
Troppo—Too much. *Allegro ma non troppo*—Not too **quickly.**

Volti subito, V.S.—Turn over the page quickly.

RELATING TO INTENSITY.

Crescendo (cres.)—Becoming louder.

Decrescendo (decres.), Diminuendo (dim.)—Becoming **softer.**

Forte (f)—Loud.
Fortissimo (ff)—Very loud.

Mezzo forte (mf)—Moderately loud.
Mezzo piano (mp)—Moderately soft.

Piano (p)—Soft.
Pianissimo (pp)—Very soft.
Forte-piano (fp)—Indicates a short forceful accent.

Calando—Gradually becoming softer and slower.

Mancando
Morendo ⎫
Perdendosi ⎬ Dying away.
Smorzando ⎭
Sforzando, Forzato—Similar to *fp*.

44

IN REFERENCE TO INSTRUMENTS.

(a) Pianoforte.

Una corda—Lit. ' One string ', i.e., use the left pedal.

Tre corde—Release (take up) the left pedal.

Pedale or *Ped.*—Use the right-hand (damper) pedal.

M.D. (*Mano destra*)—Use the right hand.

M.G. (*Main gauche*)
M.S. (*Mano sinistra*) } Use the left hand.

(b) Violin.

Pizzicato (*pizz.*)—Pluck the strings with the finger instead of using the bow.

Arco—Use the bow again.

Con sordino(*i*)—With mute(s).

Senza sordino(*i*)—Without mute(s).

Sul ponticello—(With the bow) near the bridge.

Sul G—Play on the G string only.

⊔ or ⊓ —Down bow.　V —Up bow.

Divisi—A direction for a group of instruments which normally play the same notes together, e.g., 1st violins, 2nd violins, etc., to divide and play in two or more parts.

SOME GERMAN TERMS USED IN MUSIC.

Aber—But.

Bewegt, Beweglich—With movement.

Breit—Broadly.

Einfach—Simply.

Gehalten—Sustained.

Immer—Always, throughout.

Langsam—Slowly.

Lebhaft—Lively.

Mässig—Moderately.

Noch—Still more.

Rasch—Quickly.

Ruhig—Calmly.

Schnell—Quickly.

Sehr—Very.

Stark—Loudly, forcibly.

Wenig—A little, rather.

Ziemlich—Rather, moderately.

EXERCISES

Use of Clefs

1. Prefix a clef before each of these notes so that in each case the note is A.

2. Write the following melody (a) on the Alto stave, (b) on the Tenor stave, maintaining the given pitch of the notes:

BRAHMS.

3. Rewrite the following passage in the Treble (G) clef:

PALESTRINA.

Ple - ni sunt coe - li et ter - ra.

4. Write the following melody at the same pitch in the ways indicated.

MOZART. Requiem.

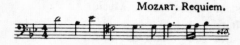

(a) For Tenor voice, using the C clef.
(b) For Alto voice, using the C clef.

Scales and Intervals

1. Show the difference in formation between a Major scale and its Tonic Minor (both forms).

2. Name the seven degrees of the scale and explain the nomenclature adopted.

3. Write one octave (ascending) of each of the following scales in quavers. Use the Bass clef, prefixing key-signatures:

(a) E♮ Melodic minor.
(b) Harmonic Chromatic of G minor.

(c) Db major.
(d) Ab Melodic Chromatic (Major key).
(e) B minor (Harmonic form).

4. Name the keys with the following signatures:

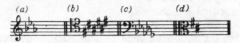

5. Write the following scales without using key-signatures:
   (i) F minor: Melodic form (ascending).
   (ii) E minor: Harmonic form (descending).
   (iii) D minor (Harmonic).
   (iv) Ab minor (Melodic) descending.

6. Name the intervals in the following:

7. Name the following intervals and write out the scale of a key in which each might occur:

8. Name the following intervals and the keys in which they are found:

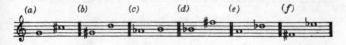

Enharmonically change *one* of the notes in each of the above and then re-name the intervals.

47

9. Write the following harmonic intervals in minims **on the** Bass staff:

(a) Perfect 5th below F♯.
(b) Diminished 7th above G♮.
(c) Major 3rd below E♭.
(d) Augmented 4th above B♭.
(e) Minor 6th below D♯.

10. Write the following melodic intervals in quavers on the Tenor staff, joining stems:

(a) Augmented 2nd below C♯.
(b) Diminished 4th above F♯.
(c) Major 3rd below E♯.
(d) Major 7th above A♯.

11. Write:

(a) An Augmented 4th above B, using the Alto staff.
(b) A Minor 6th below D, using the Soprano staff. (*See footnote*, p. 5)
(c) A Diminished 7th above E, using the Treble staff.
(d) The scale of E minor (melodic form), beginning on the Mediant, using the Tenor staff.

12. (a) Write the scale of the key in which the following phrase is written, and name the intervals between each note of the phrase and the next note.

(b) Rewrite the phrase an octave lower, using the Alto clef.
(c) Transpose the phrase into the key which is a Minor 3rd lower and write in the Treble clef.

13. In what key is the following passage? Give your reasons.

14. Name the inversions of these intervals:

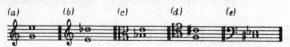

15. Write the key-signatures of E Minor, G♯ minor, F♯ minor on the Treble staff. Also name the keys in which the following intervals can be found:

Transposition

1. Transpose this passage to the key of G.

2. Transpose the following:
(a) to the key a Major 3rd higher.

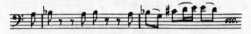

(b) to the key an Augmented 4th higher.

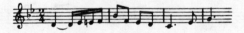

3. (a) Transpose to the key a Minor 3rd higher.

(b) Rewrite the given phrase an octave lower, using the Alto clef.

4. Transpose the given melody a Diminished 5th lower, using the Alto clef. Bar the transposed version, name its key- and time-signatures, and insert the bar lines.

5. Transpose the following a Major 3rd down:

Transcription

1. Transcribe the following extract into short score, at the same time transposing it up a Minor 3rd. State the keys through which the music passes, both in the original example and in the transposed versions.

J. S. BACH.

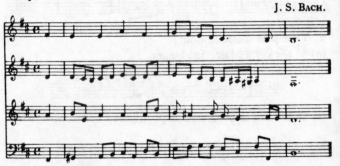

2. Transcribe into short score, at the same time transposing it down an Augmented second.

MENDELSSOHN. 'St Paul.'

Time-Signatures: Grouping of notes and rests

1. Explain the difference between Simple and Compound time.
2. Bar the following and add time-signatures.

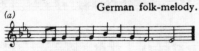

German folk-melody.

Russian.

(c)

(d) (e) Greek.

3. Bar the following in accordance with the time-signature:

4. Bar the following in $\frac{3}{8}$ time; then rewrite in notes of double value and add the time-signature.

5. Add time-signatures and bar lines to the following. Give your reasons for the barring you adopt.

(a)

(b)

6. Bar the following, adding the time-signature:

(a)

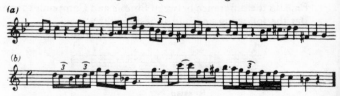

(b)

7. Correct the grouping of the notes or of the rests in the following:

(a)   *(b)*

(c)   *(d)*

(e)   *(f)*

(g   *(h)*

(i)   *(j)*

8. Complete the following bars with rests:

(a)   *(b)*

(c)   *(d)*

(e)

9. Complete the following bars with rests:

(a)   *(b)*   *(c)*

10. Rewrite the following so that the effect remains unchanged:

(a) In Simple time.

HANDEL. ' Acis and Galatea.

(i)

MENDELSSOHN. 'Lieder ohne Worte.'

(ii)

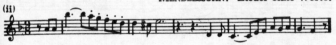

(b) In Compound time.

BACH. Organ Prelude, ' In dulci Jubilo.'

(i)

BEETHOVEN. Pianoforte Sonata.

(ii)

Ornaments

1. Write out the following passages as they are to be played:

(a) *Allegro*   BEETHOVEN.

(b) *Allegretto*   BACH.

(c) *Allegro*   BACH.

(d) *Allegro*   BEETHOVEN.

2. Write out the following passages in full:

(a) *Allegro con brio*   BEETHOVEN.

(b) *Allegro*   MOZART.   (c) *Moderato*   BACH.

(d) *Andante cantabile*   BACH.

3. Write out the following ornaments, etc., as they would be performed:

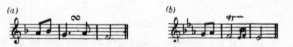

(a)   (b)

4. Write out the following passages in full:

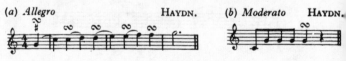

(a) *Allegro*   HAYDN.   (b) *Moderato*   HAYDN.

54

(c) *Allegro* BEETHOVEN.

(d) *Adagio* HAYDN.

(e) *Allegro* MOZART.

(f) *Moderato* COUPERIN.

Terms and Abbreviations

1. Explain the following terms: (a) tre corde; (b) morendo; (c) cantabile; (d) tenuto; (e) con brio.
What are the uses of the following signs?

(a) ———   (b) ⊤̣   (c) 𝄢   (d) Met. 96   (e) ⊓ V

2. What do you understand by the term *Syncopation?* Show three methods of producing it. Illustrate your answer in ⁶⁄₈ time.

3. Give an example of each of the following:

(a) Chromatic semitone, (b) Diatonic semitone, (c) Tritone, (d) Enharmonic change, (e) Tetrachord.

4. Explain the terms:
Alla breve, Common time, Compound-triple time.

5. Give the English equivalents of:

(a) Andantino, (b) Calando, (c) Mezzo-staccato, (d) Pizzicato, (e) Con sordini, (f) Stringendo, (g) Tempo rubato, (h) Una corda, (i) Giocoso, (j) Colla voce.

CHAPTER II

Melody Writing

1. In the following melodies the phrases show a simple arrangement A A B A.

The only essential difference between the two melodies is that in (i) the phrases are each of two bars, whilst in (ii) they are twice as long.

2. This suggests a useful method for writing a melody.
First take a simple idea such as the following:

Then repeat it (with modification if necessary).

56

Now add a contrasting phrase to balance the above.

Complete the melody by adding the first phrase A in its original form or slightly modified.

Notice that in each phrase the incomplete bar at the end, together with the part of a bar at the beginning, makes one complete bar.

For the present, it will be well to commence with a note of the Tonic chord and to end with the Tonic. *As a general rule*, however, do not end any phrase with the Tonic, except the last.

PHRASE BUILDING

3. In building phrases use three kinds of movement, viz.:
(*a*) *Conjunct*, i.e., movement by step.

(*b*) *Disjunct*, movement by leap (a Major or Minor 3rd; Perfect 4th or 5th, etc.).

A wider leap may be taken if it be approached and quitted within the interval:

Avoid difficult leaps such as the Augmented 2nd, the Augmented 4th, the *Major* 7th, and compound intervals. The Diminished 5th may be used if approached and quitted within the interval.

(*c*) *Repetition of the same note.* This should only be used when it gives character to a phrase.

Nun danket Alle.

In writing a melody, vary the movement. A good rule is ' after stepping take a leap, after leaping take a step '.

4. A phrase should have both melodic curve and rhythm, thus:

    (*a*) Curve only.   (*b*) Rhythm only.

Rhythm *and* melodic curve.

BRAHMS. String Sextet, Op. 36.

Exercises 1 and 2 at the end of this chapter should now be worked.

5. *Modification of the simple A A B A plan.*
First Modification.

Instead of the first phrase being repeated at the same pitch, it may be repeated in *sequence*, i.e., at another pitch.

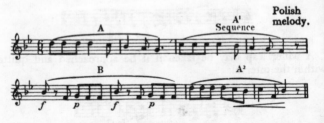

The last phrase, A², is simply A modified.

Second Modification.

The phrase A instead of being repeated, may be *inverted*:

Phrase:

Inversion:

Inversion of a phrase need not be exact: a leap of a 4th or a 6th may be taken instead of a 5th, etc., if it makes a better melodic line.

(a) 5th

(b) Inversion of *(a)* 4th

Melody by Inversion.

A   A' (Inversion of A)

B   A

Work Exercise 3.

6. *The A B B A plan.*

Still keeping to melodies with four phrases, we may now adopt another arrangement thus: **A B B A.**

A   B   Border tune.

B'   A'

A perfect example of this pattern is the well-known 'Lincoln-shire Poacher'.

The Lincolnshire Poacher.

In order to make sure of a satisfactory balance and continuity of phrases, it will be well to end the first phrase A with the Tonic, and the phrase B with a note other than the Tonic.

Work Exercises 4 and 5.

7. *Balance of Phrases*.

When, as in the above case, the phrases are made up of sub-phrases, these must be balanced in one of the following ways:

(i) By direct repetition.

Polish melody

(ii) By means of *Sequence*.

German.

(iii) By *repartee*, or contrast.

Hungarian.

Work exercises 6, 7, 8.

8. *Other Patterns used in Melody Writing*.

Melodies should now be attempted with other patterns besides A A B A and A B B A. Such patterns vary from

A B C D, in which all the phrases are different, to A A A A in which the same idea is used for each phrase.

The following are examples of melodies illustrating the various patterns.

(i) *A B A B.*

Dutch melody.

(ii) *A B A C.*

Mozart.

(iii) *A A A B.*
Variation of the A phrase adds to the melodic interest.

' Good Morrow, 'tis St Valentine's Day.'

(iv) *A A A A.*

Irish Folk Tune.

Work exercises 9 and 10.

9. *Change of key in Melody.*

It is sometimes felt that a phrase of a melody leads naturally into a new key. In that case the melody must always return and end in the original key. Modulation may be indicated clearly or merely implied.

Modulation to the Dominant.

'The Blue Bell of Scotland.'

Implied modulation to Dominant.

' The Vicar of Bray.'

The modulations most frequently found are those to the Dominant (as in the above cases) or to the Relative major.

Hungarian

A tune may also modulate from a major key to its Relative minor, or to the Subdominant.

(*a*) *To the Relative minor.*

'I Blas Gogerddan.' Welsh melody.

(*b*) *To the Subdominant.*

' Lisa Lân.' Welsh melody.

In view of the strong feeling of new tonality, and consequent difficulty in re-establishing the home key, this modulation should be used with discretion. It will generally be effective as an incidental modulation in the second half of a melody, using the following cycle of keys:

TONIC → Rel. maj. or min. → DOMINANT → Subdominant → TONIC, or:

TONIC → Dominant → REL. MAJOR or MINOR → Subdominant → TONIC.

There is no fixed rule as to where modulation will occur. It will be sufficient here to notice that in tunes constructed

A A B A, modulation frequently takes place in the B phrase, whilst in others (A B A B, A B C D, etc.) it will occur at the end of the first half. (See p. 70 re Binary tunes.)

Work exercises 11, 12, 13.

10. *Completion or elaboration of melodic outline.*

It will often be found possible to elaborate the outline by means of passing-notes, arpeggio notes, etc.*; the implied harmony should be borne in mind when using these devices.

(*a*) Plain outline of melody.

(*b*) Elaborated outline.

Passing notes
Arpeggio note

In writing passing-notes, divide the *weak* rather than the strong beats.

Other decorative devices.

Outline

Decorated

upper Auxiliary note
lower Auxiliary note

Outline

Decorated

lower Auxiliary note
Appoggiatura
Accented passing note

* See pp. 87, 124.

Changing-notes.

These may be used to decorate a single *essential* note*, being taken a step above and below, and returning to the essential note.

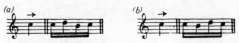

They may also be taken between two essential notes a third apart†:

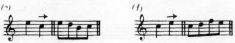

The first changing-note is taken by step and proceeds by a third in the same direction, returning by step to the second essential note.

Work exercise 14.

11. *Extension of phrase-length.*

Extension of the normal phrase-length should be practised freely, since it makes for greater rhythmic variety. The following are the chief devices:

(i) Repetition of a note, or notes belonging to the cadence, with or without modification.

HAYDN. Pianoforte Sonata (end).

BEETHOVEN. Symphony No. 5 in C minor.

* *Essential* note, i.e., one which would be regarded as a chord-note if the melody were harmonized.

† They then form a *Nota Cambiata*.

(ii) Lengthening a note either leading to, or being part of the cadence.

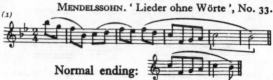

MENDELSSOHN. ' Lieder ohne Wörte ', No. 33.

(1)

Normal ending:

(b)

WAGNER. ' Lohengrin.'

(iii) Temporarily averting the final cadence, with or without repetition of the whole or part of the phrase which would have led to it.

French melody.

(a)

Extension

(b)

HAYDN. Quartet, Op. 3, No. 6.

Extension by repetition

(iv) Repeating a bar or more, with or without sequence.

HAYDN. Quartet, Op. 1, No. 6.

(a)

(b) Minuetto

Sequential repetition

12. *Melodic Climax*

A good melody will generally be found to have some point of climax occurring at the summit of its melodic curve, or reached through its highest note; this should therefore be kept for an after-phrase, or even for the very end as in ' God Save the King ' or ' The Marseillaise '. The important thing is that the growth of a melody should be logical, and that the climax be reached through a succession of rising phrases or some form of cumulative device such as repetition or sequence. The following melodies should be studied from these standpoints.

(a) **Rising Phrases.**

' Barbara Allen.'

(b) **Repetition.**

' Ye Banks and Braes.'

(c) Sequence leading to Climax.

MORLEY. ' It was a Lover and his Lass.'

13. *Contraction of Sentences**.

(i) By overlapping the end of one phrase and the beginning of the next.

SCHUBERT. Violin and Pianoforte Sonatina in D

(ii) Omission of a phrase.
(a) Normal eight-bar sentence.

(b) Six-bar sentence due to omission.

French melody

(iii) Omission of *part* of phrase.
(a) Normal eight-bar sentence.

(b) Seven-bar sentence—by omission.

* See Chap. VI, p. 185.

68

Work exercises 15, 16, and 17.

14. *Use of other scales.*

It is not necessary that we should confine ourselves to the modern major and minor scales. Other 'scales' such as the *Pentatonic*, the *Hexachord*, and the *Dorian mode* can often be used with advantage. In such a case, use the notes of one particular scale or mode for the whole melody thus:

(*a*) Hexachord   Example   'Robin Adair.'

(*b*) Pentatonic Scale   Example in Pentatonic Scale 'Auld Lang Syne.'

(*c*) Dorian Mode   Example in Dorian Mode

15. *Writing a melody by Condensation.*

Take a phrase (*a*) and balance it by Contrast.

Repeat the above at the same or a different pitch.

Add (*b*) and repeat: follow with (½*b*), etc.

69

This gives:

16. *Melodies in Binary and Ternary Form.*
(i) *Binary Form.*

The first half (A) of a Binary melody ends generally in the key of the Dominant, or in the relative major or minor.

The second half may commence in the home key or in the new key; but do not use the actual opening bars of the melody at the beginning of the second half, except in the new key.

(a)   'Farewell, Manchester!'

Reprinted from the National Song-book, by permission of Messrs Boosey and Co., Ltd.

(b)

Note the use made of the opening phrase at the commencement of the second half; and also the transposition of the second half of A (modified) in the last phrase.

(ii) *Ternary Form*.

A melody in Ternary form has three sections, viz., A B A'. The first should, strictly, be complete in itself : the second is a contrasting section, and the third recapitulates the first, with or without modification, ending in the Tonic.

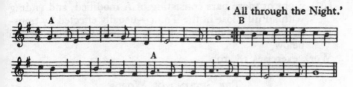

'All through the Night.'

Suggested plan for a melody in Ternary Form.
- (A) Eight bars ending in the Tonic.
- (B) Eight bars modulating through the relative minor or major to the Dominant with or without new material and sequence, and ending with the Dominant of the home key.
- (A') Recapitulation of A with or without modification and extension.

17. *Melodies in Minuet Style*.

These will be in $\frac{3}{4}$ time commencing, preferably, on the third beat of the bar.

MOZART. Minuet in D, K.94.

Suggested plan for practice*.

(A) Eight bars modulating to the Dominant.

(B) Eight bars (or possibly *four* only) using material taken from A, passing through new keys on the flat side of the Tonic, and ending with the Dominant of the home key.

(A¹) Eight or more bars consisting of A modified, and ending with a Full Close in the Tonic—usually effected by transposing the second half of A, a Perfect 4th above or 5th below.

Work exercises 18, 19.

THE SETTING OF WORDS

1. In setting words to music, the natural *speech* rhythm of the words has to be translated into the rhythm of music.

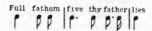

The speech rhythm is not, generally speaking, the same as the metre:

$$\cup \;\; - \cup \;\; - \;\; \cup \; - \cup \;\; -$$
Full fathom five thy father lies

2. It is desirable that a melody should suggest the mood of the words in addition to reproducing the correct speech rhythm.

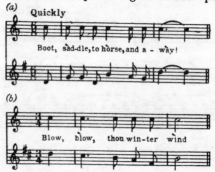

* Strictly, of course, a Minuet melody may be in **Binary** *or* **Ternary**, or even Rondo form; *vide* p. 189.

3. The steps in the setting of a stanza to music are as follows:

(*a*) Read through the lines, noting the accented syllables.

Old Meg she was a Gipsy,
And lived upon the moors:
Her bed it was the brown heath turf,
And her house was out of doors.

(*b*) Write the words between two empty staves, indicating the accent by means of short lines drawn as shown.

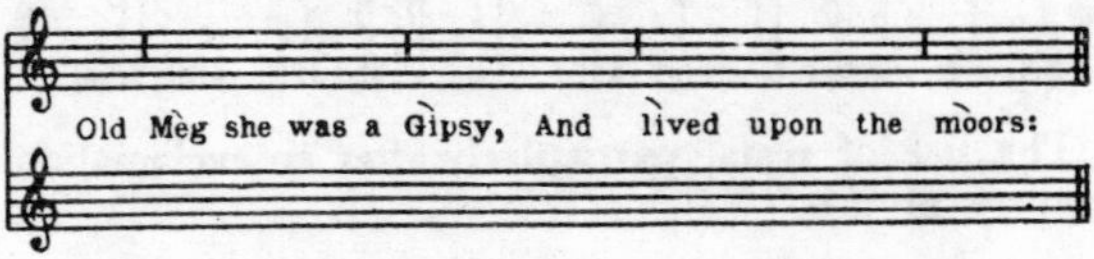

(*c*) Decide where the ***strongest*** accents occur and draw bar-lines at these places: then fill in the rhythm demanded by the words.

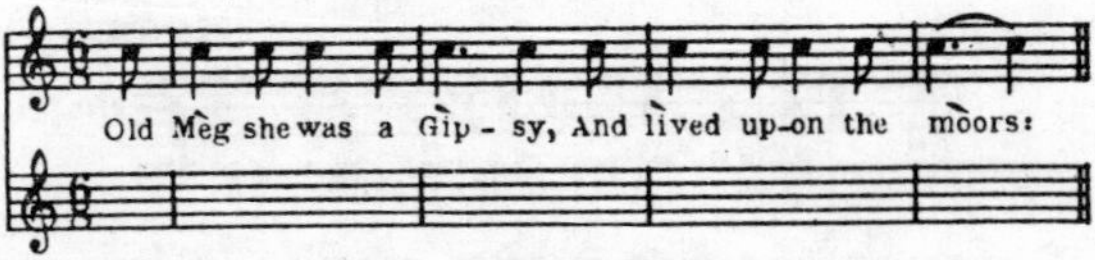

(*d*) Fill in the melodic outline, reproducing as far as possible the poetic climax of the words; this will probably be felt to occur towards the end of the third line.

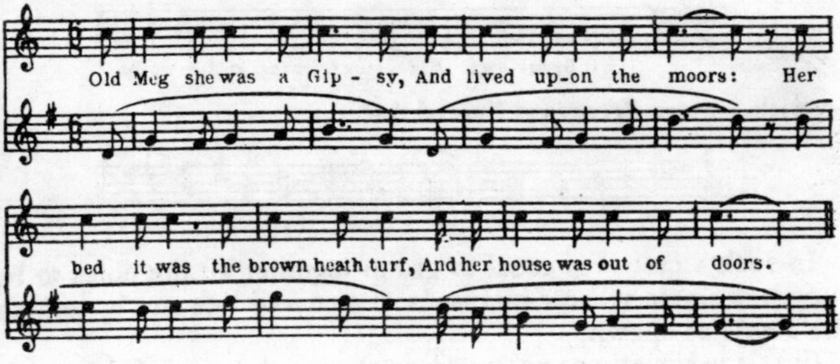

The following points should be noticed:

(i) No *unaccented* syllable should be stressed by being set to a strong accent of the music. The following is bad:

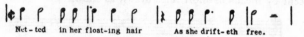

Net - ted in her float - ing hair   As she drift - eth free.

and should be amended thus:

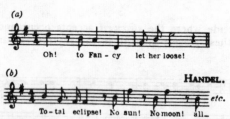

Net - ted in her float - ing hair   As she drift - eth free.

(ii) The use of rests, particularly after an exclamation or an exclamatory phrase.

(a)

Oh!   to Fan - cy   let her loose!

(b)

HANDEL.

To - tal eclipse! No sun! No moon! all— *etc.*

(iii) Decoration of a note is often effective in improving the melodic line. Thus the words:

' O Swallow! Flying from the golden woods '

might be set with correct speech-rhythm thus:

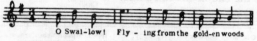

O Swal-low!   Fly - ing from the gold-en woods

or with a more decorated line of melody:

O Swal-low!   Fly - ing from the gold-en woods

In such a case it is usual to group together all the notes to be sung to a single syllable by means of a curved line and by joining the stems as shown.

(iv) It is sometimes necessary to change the *time* of the music in the course of a poem or stanza.

Thus, in Ariel's song:

> Where the bee sucks, there suck I,
> In a Cowslip's bed I lie.
>
> Merrily, merrily shall I live now
> Under the blossom that hangs on the bough.

the rhythm suggested by the words is as follows:

Example of the setting of words.

> Have you seen but a white Lily grow
> Before rude hands had touch'd it?
> Have you marked the fall of the snow
> Before the earth hath smutch'd it?

In the following, the upper line gives the simple speech-rhythm and the lower line the decorated form of the same rhythm.

Anon.

The same considerations apply to a six- or eight-line stanza, or even to a whole poem. It will be well to think out a definite key scheme beforehand as suggested by the form and content of the words.

EXERCISES

1. Complete the phrases, using the rhythm indicated:

2. Add a melodic outline to each of the following:

3. Complete the following as melodies, using the given patterns:

4. Complete the following as eight-bar melodies:

Rewrite the melody obtained from ii, making **B¹** in sequence with **B**.

5. Expand the following melody to eight bars:

6. Write a melody of eight bars, beginning as follows:

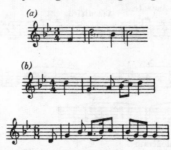

7. Write a melody in the key indicated, to fit the following rhythm:

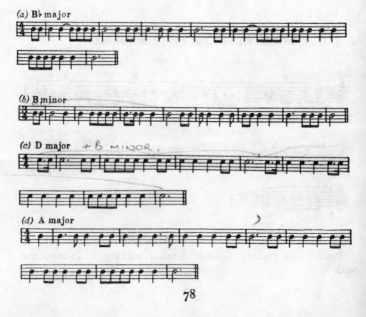

(a) Bb major

(b) B minor

(c) D major + B MINOR,

(d) A major

8. Write a melody upon the given plan, modulating (a) to the Dominant, (b) to the Relative minor, and ending, in each case, in the Tonic.

9. Continue the following for about fourteen bars:

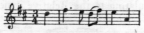

10. Beginning as follows, write melodies, introducing any variations of the normal patterns you choose:

11. Begin as follows, and continue in a well-balanced manner. Introduce simple modulation.

12. Continue the following by adding a responsive phrase: a) ending in the Relative major, (b) in the Dominant, (c) ending n the Subdominant.

13. Add a responsive phrase to the following: (a) ending in G major, (b) ending in A minor, (c) ending in D major.

14. Write short melodies beginning as follows:
(a) In Binary form.   (b) In Ternary form.

(c) Binary, modulating to the Relative major.

(d) Ternary, modulating to Dominant.

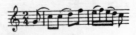

15. Extend the following melodies:
(a) By Cadential repetition:

Extension

(b) By repeating a middle phrase in sequence:

16. Complete the following as eight-bar melodies, introducing an inverted form of A or B, or both:

17. Rewrite the following as a six-bar sentence by omitting a phrase:

18. Write a melody in Minuet style. Begin thus:

19. Using the given material, write a melody by condensation.

EXERCISES IN THE SETTING OF WORDS

1. Write a monotone in Staff notation suitable to the rhythm of the following:

(a)   My heart leaps up when I behold
       A rainbow in the sky.—WORDSWORTH.

(b)   Toll for the brave!
       The brave that are no more!—COWPER.

(c)   Oh, to be in England now that April's there,
        And whoever wakes in England sees, some morning,
            unaware.—R. BROWNING.

(d)   In the moonlight the shepherds,
        Soft lull'd by the rills,
      Lie wrapt in their blankets,
        Asleep on the hills.—M. ARNOLD.

(e)   The slender acacia would not shake
        One long milk bloom on the tree;
      The white lake-blossom fell into the lake
        As the primrose dozed on the lea.—TENNYSON.

2. Set the following words to music, paying particular regard
to the speech-rhythms and choosing your own patterns for the
melodies.

(a)   Gone were but the winter cold,
        And gone were but the snow,
      I could sleep in the wild woods
        Where primroses blow.—ALLAN CUNNINGHAM.

(b)   Bards of Passion and of Mirth,
      Ye have left your souls on earth!
      Have ye souls in heaven too,
      Double-lived in regions new?—KEATS.

(c)   Flow down, cold rivulet, to the sea,
        Thy tribute wave deliver:
      No more by thee my steps shall be,
        For ever and for ever.—TENNYSON.

(d)   I too will something make
        And joy in the making;
      Altho' to-morrow it seem
      Like the empty words of a dream
        Remembered on waking.—R. BRIDGES.

(e)   Charm me asleep, and melt me so
        With thy delicious numbers;
      That being ravisht, hence I goe
        Away in easie slumbers.—HERRICK.

(f)

Hie upon Hielands, and laigh upon Tay,
Bonnie George Campbell rade out on a day;
Saddled, and bridled, and gallant rade he;
Hame cam' his guid horse, but never cam' he.

ANON.

(g)

The soul of music slumbers in its shell
Till waked and kindled by the master's spell;
And feeling hearts, touch them but rightly, pour
A thousand melodies unheard before.—ROGERS.

(h)

The upper air burst into life!
And a hundred fire-flags sheen,
To and fro, they were hurried about;
And to and fro, and in and out,
The wan stars danced between.—COLERIDGE.

(i)

What was he doing, the great god Pan,
    Down in the reeds by the river?
Spreading ruin and scattering ban,
    Splashing and paddling with hoofs of a goat,
    And breaking the golden lilies afloat
    With the dragon-fly on the river.

E. B. BROWNING.

(j)

Awake! for morning in the Bowl of Night
Has flung the Stone that puts the Stars to Flight:
    And Lo! the Hunter of the East has caught
The Sultan's Turret in a Noose of Light.

TAMAM SHUD (*trans.* FITZGERALD).

(k)

Seamen three! What men be ye?
    Gotham's three wise men we be.
Whither in your bowl so free?
    To rake the moon from out the sea.
The bowl goes trim. The moon doth shine
And our ballast is old wine
And your ballast is old wine.—PEACOCK.

83

(l)   ' And the people from the margin
Watched him floating, rising, sinking,
Till the birch canoe seemed lifted
High into that sea of splendour,
Till it sank into the vapours
Like the new moon slowly, slowly
Sinking in the purple distance.
                    LONGFELLOW, ' Hiawatha's Departure '.

(m)   Up the airy mountain,
            Down the rushy glen,
We daren't go a-hunting
            For fear of little men;
Wee folk, good folk,
            Trooping all together;
Green jacket, red cap,
            And white owl's feather !
                    WILLIAM ALLINGHAM (*set in C.L. Exam.*).

(n)   The winds, as at their hour of birth,
            Leaning upon the ridged sea,
Breathed low around the rolling earth
            With mellow preludes, ' We are free '.
The streams thro' many a lilied row
            Down-carolling to the crisped sea,
Low-tinkled with a bell-like flow
            Atween the blossoms, ' We are free '.
                    TENNYSON (*set in C.L. Exam.*)

84

CHAPTER III

TWO-PART WRITING

(This chapter should be taken in conjunction with Chapter IV)

1. In two-part writing it is important that each part should make a good melodic line.

HANDEL. ' Acis and Galatea.'

2. The following intervals may be used:
 (i) Major and Minor 3rds and 6ths.
 (ii) The Unison and Octave, and the Perfect 5th.
Both parts should end with notes of the Tonic chord (*vide* Chap. IV, p. 96).

3. It will be well to aim at contrary motion between the parts and not to have more than three 3rds or three 6ths in succession. Do not use consecutive *major* thirds except with the parts moving a semitone:

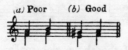

The use of consecutive 5ths and octaves is forbidden.

4. The Octave (or unison) may be used as follows:
 (i) At the beginning, or the ending, or both.
 (ii) On the Dominant of the final cadence (*vide* example, par. 1).

(iii) *On a weak beat.*

(*a*) Between two positions of the same chord, both parts moving by step, and in contrary motion.

(*b*) When the notes forming the octave belong to the same chord as that used on the previous strong beat.

5. The Perfect 5th may be used:
(i) *At the beginning, over the Tonic or Dominant.*

(ii) *On a weak beat* when the upper part moves by step between the Tonic and the Mediant or *vice versa*, or between the Subdominant and the Submediant.

The inversions of the above also make good harmony, and may be freely used.

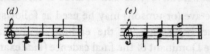

86

(iii) *On the Dominant of the final cadence.*

6. Parts may be written on separate staves, or together on a single stave; in the latter case the notes of the upper part will have their stems turned upwards, those of the lower part downwards.

7. It will not always be necessary, or even desirable, that the parts be written note for note with each other.

At (*a*) all three notes of the melody belong to the chord of G major, and may be regarded as arpeggio notes; at (*b*) we have C and A as passing-notes, i.e., notes proceeding by step between two chord notes a third apart*.

Note also the following devices:

(i) *Use of Auxiliary notes.*

Upper auxiliary note.   *Lower* auxiliary notes.

An *upper* auxiliary note is that next above a chord note, and belonging to the scale commencing with the *root* of the chord.

A *lower* auxiliary note is usually one semitone below the chord note as in (*b*) and (*c*).

(ii) *Use of accented passing notes, suspensions, etc.* (See Chapter IV, Sections VIII and XI.)

* Strictly, they are both essential notes derived from the Dominant chords.

8. *Examples.*

  (i) *Part added note for note with the melody.*

SCHUBERT. 'The Spendthrift Spring.'

  (ii) *Added part commences after the melody.*

MOZART. Minuet in D, K.94.

etc.

(iii) *Upper part added.*

(The same principles apply. First sketch out the part to be added and decorate it, if necessary.)

(a) Sketch

Given bass

(b) Completed

MOZART. K.4.

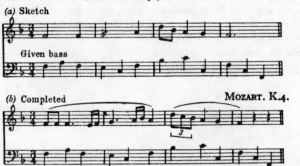

  (iv) Crossing of parts in order to enhance the melodic interest: this should be used sparingly.

Oxford Folk-Song Series, Book IX, No. 28.

WRITING FOR STRINGED INSTRUMENTS

String writing should now be practised in two parts. The following points should be noticed.

1. *Compass of the instruments.*

Care must be taken to write within the compass of each instrument. Higher notes than the above are possible in each case, but these will not usually be necessary.

2. When any of these instruments are played together, the violin takes the upper part and the viola or 'cello the lower. The treatment of each part is usually freer than with voices.

BEETHOVEN. Trio in D major, Op. 8. Serenade.

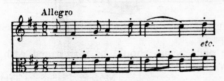

3. Notes intended to be played with one bow (i.e., one *stroke* of the bow) are written with a slur ⌣.

MOZART. Symphony in G minor.

(*a*) Dots written above each of the slurred notes indicate that the notes are to be slightly detached by playing them with small portions of the same bow.

BEETHOVEN. String Quartet, Op. 18, No. 5.

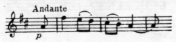

(*b*) Slight emphasis to be placed on each of the slurred notes is shown thus:

DVOŘÁK. Pianoforte Quintet, Op. 81.

(*c*) Normally, a *down* bow will begin on a strong beat, but when there is an anacrusis* it will often begin before.

BEETHOVEN. Symphony No. 1.

(⊓ or ⊔ represents a *down* bow; V an *up* bow.)

(*d*) A note being the end of a scale passage, and occurring on the first beat of the bar, should be played with the same bow as the preceding notes.

STRAUSS. ' Don Quixote.'

4. The use of figuration helps materially in producing interesting string parts.

A figure once begun should be maintained with reasonable consistency.

MOZART. Pianoforte Trio in G major.

5. Generally speaking, it will be better, if one part commences with an anacrusis, for the second to commence similarly.

MOZART. Pianoforte Trio in G major.

* *Anacrusis*, the linking of *weak to strong accent*, usually at the beginning of a section or phrase.

6. Strings are sometimes plucked with the fingers instead of being played with the bow; this is called *pizzicato*, and is indicated by the abbreviation *pizz.* written above each part to be thus played. Resumption of the use of the bow is indicated by the word *arco*.

7. Strings may be muted in order to reduce and alter their tone. The use of the mute is indicated by the words *con sordino*, and its removal by *senza sordino*. Sufficient time must be allowed by means of rests in the written part to enable the player to place the mute or to remove it, as the case may be.

EXERCISES

1. Add a second part below each of the following, note for note of the melody. Write both parts on the same stave.

2. Elaborate the upper part of the following:

(*a*) Using passing notes.

(*b*) Using auxiliary notes.

3. Elaborate the lower part in the following, using arpeggio notes.

4. Write a part above each of the following:

5. Below the given melody write a part moving in crotchets for the Bass voice.

6. Add a suitable violin part to the given 'cello part.

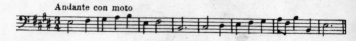

7. Complete the following for two parts:

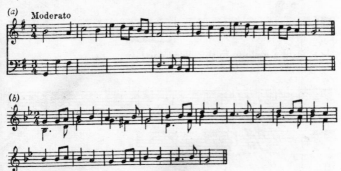

(a) Moderato

8. Add a part for violoncello below this for violin:

9. Above this Bass, and in the Treble clef, write a melody in the rhythm indicated.

(a)

(b)

10. Add a melodious Tenor part to the following:

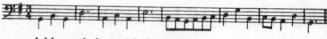

11. Add a melody to this Bass part:

(a)

(b)

12. Below the given melody write a flowing part for the Bass voice.

13. Write a simple part for the Bass voice below the given Carol melody.

14. Add a Treble part above the following Bass:

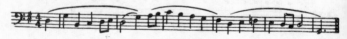

94

15. Write a part for Violin above the given 'Cello part . . . the rhythm of the added part should vary from that of the given part.

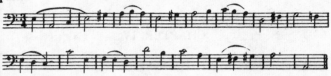

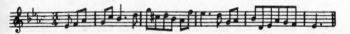

16. Add a Bass part to the following:
    (a)

    (b)

17. Write an interesting Alto part below the following melody:

18. Add a Bass part to the following melody:

19. Add an Alto part to the following melody:

CHAPTER IV

HARMONY

I—The Primary Triads of a Major Key

1. A combination of sounds consisting of a note (the *Root*) with the 3rd and the 5th above it constitutes a *Triad* or *Chord*.

If the 3rd be omitted the combination sounds bare and unfinished.

2. A triad can be formed on each degree of the scale, and takes the name of the note upon which it is built, e.g., *Tonic* chord, *Dominant*, etc.

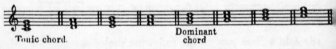

Tonic chord.   Dominant
                                        chord

3. The triads on the Tonic, Subdominant and Dominant are the *Primary triads* of the key. Each has a Major 3rd and a Perfect 5th from the root and is therefore called a *Major Common Chord*.

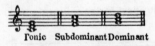

Tonic   Subdominant Dominant

4. Roman numerals are used to denote *Major* Common Chords thus: I=Tonic chord; IV=Subdominant; V=Dominant*.

* The notation for other chords is given on pp. 105, 108, 149.

96

5. The relative positions of the 3rd and 5th may be changed provided that no two *upper* parts are more than an octave apart. The root must, for the present, remain to be the lowest note.

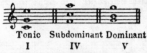

Tonic   Subdominant Dominant
  I   IV   V

6. An interval greater than an octave may occur between the Bass (the lowest note) and the note next above it.

Tonic   Subdominant Dominant

7. When writing for *four* voices it becomes necessary to double one of the notes. This may be done at the Unison or the Octave. Either the root or the 5th of a primary triad may be doubled, but *not* the Major 3rd.

Root doubled 5th   Root   5th   Root   5th

8. A chord may be written without its 5th but not without the 3rd.

Incorrect

9. Arrange chords for the present as if for voices. If the note have stems these should be turned upwards for the Soprano an Tenor, and downwards for the Alto and Bass—the highest no being written for the Soprano, the next for Alto, etc.

The approximate compass of each voice is as follows:

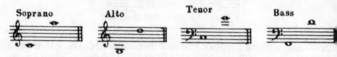

10. Avoid having the 3rd of a chord lower than E belo Middle C, the effect is cloudy and unpleasant.

11. The following are arrangements of the three Primar triads in G major and F major.

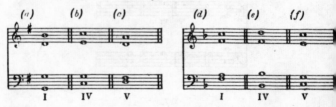

1. Write a Major Common Chord on each of the following notes. Name each one.

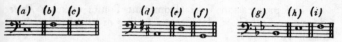

2. By adding a note for the Soprano, complete the following as major chords for four voices.

3. Fill in the missing notes:

4. Harmonize each of the following in *two ways*:

II—Chord Progressions. Cadences in a Major Key

1. Two chords in immediate succession produce a *harmonic progression*.

2. The progression V—I (Dominant-Tonic) makes a *Perfect Cadence* or *Full Close*. It effects a feeling of 'finality' or 'conclusion'.

Reversing the above order of chords gives an *Imperfect Cadence* or *Half Close*.

Notice the following points:

(i) The chords forming a Cadence are used from a *weak* a *strong* accent*.

(ii) The Leading note should rise to the Tonic.

(iii) A note common to two chords is kept in the *same* part an (with the exception of the Bass) the parts move as little possible.

* Otherwise a *Feminine* ending results:

3. The progression IV—I makes a *Plagal Cadence*—sometimes described as an *Amen Cadence*.

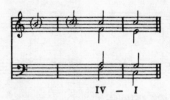

IV — I

4. Two other progressions are also available:

(a)   *(b)*

I — IV   IV — V

Ex. (*b*) is a form of Half Close.
The progression V—IV will not be used for the present.*

. Consecutive fifths and octaves.

No two parts may move in consecutive (parallel) Perfect 5ths or octaves thus:

(a)   *(b)*

* The best way to use this progression is to make the three upper parts move in contrary motion with the Bass: even then it is not always satisfactory.

[Good]

V — IV

The following progressions are therefore bad:

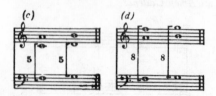

6. *Exposed fifths and octaves.*

If two outer parts approach a Perfect 5th or octave by *similar* motion the upper part should move by step, otherwise an *Exposed* 5th or octave occurs.

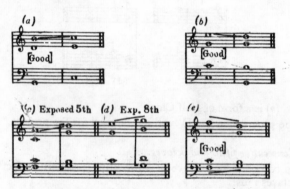

NOTE.—Exposed 5ths or octaves do not occur between two statements of the *same* chord.

7. *Crossing and Overlapping of parts.*

(*a*) Parts should not cross.

(*b*) They should not proceed to a unison by similar motion, except as in (ii) below:

(Allowed in V—I, between Tenor and Bass.)

(*c*) They should not overlap except, if necessary, between two positions of the same chord: for example, the Alto in one chord should not be higher than the Soprano of the preceding chord, or the Bass higher than the Tenor.

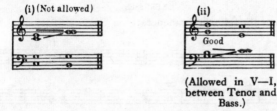

8. *Melodic progression of parts.*

No voice or part may leap a Major 7th, or an Augmented 4th, or any Compound interval.

Bad part writing.

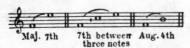

A Diminished 5th, a Sixth, or a Minor 7th or Octave, must be preceded and followed by a note *within* the interval.

Allowable.

Dim. 5th   6th   Min. 7th   8th

9. *Recommendations relating to chord progressions.*

(i) Aim at contrary motion between the outer parts.

(ii) Aim at movement to the *nearest* note in any part excepting the Bass.

EXERCISES

1. Name the following cadences:

2. Fill in Alto and Tenor parts in the following:
Perfect Cadences.

Imperfect Cadences.

Plagal Cadences.

3. Add parts for S.A.T.

4. Add A.T.B.

Name each of the cadences which you have written above.

5. Write cadences for S.A.T.B. as follows:

   (*a*) Perfect in B♭ major, D major, A major.

   (*b*) Imperfect in G major, E major, F major.

   (*c*) Plagal in E♭ major, D major, F♯ major.

III—*Primary Triads and Cadences in a Minor Key*

1. The three Primary triads of a minor key are derived from the Harmonic Minor scale. They occur on the same degrees as in the major, viz., Tonic, Subdominant, and Dominant.

The Tonic and Subdominant chords have each a Minor 3rd and a Perfect 5th from the root, and are described as *Minor Common chords*; they are denoted (i) and (iv) respectively. The Dominant (V) is a Major chord.

2. Two points call for attention:

   (*a*) The 3rd of a minor chord may be doubled freely.

   (*b*) The *Augmented 2nd* is forbidden as a melodic interval: it occurs diatonically in the Harmonic Minor scale.

3. *Cadences in the Minor.*

These are formed with the same corresponding chords as in the Major.

Perfect Cadence (V—i). Imperfect Cadence (i—V). Plagal Cadence (iv—i)

Tierce de Picardie

In the final chord of a piece in a minor key the third is sometimes sharpened, producing a ' Tierce de Picardie '.

4. *Figuring of Chords.*

A chord may be indicated by means of its Bass note, written with appropriate figuration. The progression illustrating ' Tierce de Picardie ' (above) would appear thus:

Each ♮ sign refers to the third above the Bass: other accidentals may be used similarly.

EXERCISES

1. Play the following Cadences, naming each one:

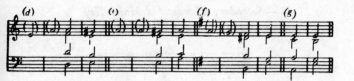

2. Fill in the Alto and Tenor parts in the following:

3. Harmonize:

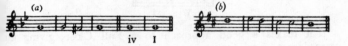

4. Write cadences for S.A.T.B. as follows:

(a) Perfect: in D minor, E minor, A minor.

(b) Imperfect: in B minor, F minor, C minor.

(c) Plagal: in F♯ minor, D minor (Tierce de Picardie), B minor.

IV—Secondary Chords of a Major Key

1. Secondary triads occur in a Major key as follows:

ii, iii, and vi are Minor Common chords, whilst that on the Leading-note is a *Diminished triad**. The notation for a Diminished triad is a small Roman numeral with a (°) as shown.

The Supertonic and the Submediant will be the only chords treated here for the present; in each of these the third, being minor, may be freely doubled.

2. The progression V—vi (weak to strong) forms an *Interrupted* or *Surprise Cadence*—also known as a *False Close*.

3. ii makes a good approach to a Full Close, giving an extra degree of solidity and conclusiveness.

* It has a *Diminished* 5th.

4. *Other forms of Half Close.*

ii — V   vi   V

5. *Suggestions relating to the choice of chords.*

(i) Roots ascending a Perfect 4th or 5th (or descending a Perfect 5th or 4th) make strong progressions.

(ii) Roots *ascending* a step of a Major 2nd are good. For the present avoid progressions *descending* a step, especially V—IV, ii—I.

(iii) Roots descending a third are good, but progressions with roots *rising* a third may only be used from a strong to a weak beat.

Good   Weak   Good

6. *Secondary chords and Exposed fifths and octaves.*

A Perfect fifth or octave between outer parts should be approached by contrary motion if one or both of the chords is a Secondary triad.

Good   Poor

The following progression is usually allowed between ii*a* an
V*a*.

7. *False relation of the Tritone.*

The effect of the following is poor because it brings the F♮
the Alto into unpleasant relationship with the B♮ of the Sopran
It produces *False relation of the Tritone**.

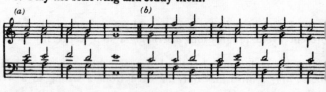

8. Play the following and study them:

9. (i) The progression V—I (Perfect Cadence) should only
used weak to strong for the *very end* and (if necessary) at t
beginning; here it merely establishes the key.

(ii) Do not precede a Full Close with the Tonic chord—o
destroys the effect of the other.

* Cf. p. 85, par. 3, *Two-part Writing.*

(iii) Change the Bass note from *weak* to *strong**:

except (if necessary) at the beginning of a phrase.

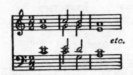

The Submediant in a Minor Key

1. VI in a minor key is a *major triad*.

2. Used after the Dominant, it forms an *Interrupted Cadence* or False Close.

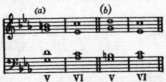

In this progression (V—VI) the Major 3rd of the Submediant must be doubled.

* A strong accent falls on the first beat of the bar in Duple or Triple time, and on the first and third beat in Quadruple time.

3. The above progression may be approached from the Sub
dominant chord or from the Tonic.

EXERCISES

1. Add A. and T. to complete the harmony for S.A.T.B.:

2. Add a Bass to the following and complete the harmony in
four parts:

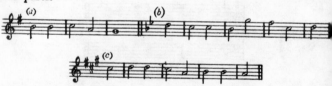

3. Add a Soprano part and complete the harmony:

4. Add inner parts for A. and T.

5. Write False Closes in D major, E♭ major, A major, G minor, F minor, C♯ minor.

6. Add a Bass and complete the harmony:

7. Add a Soprano part and complete the harmony:

8. Add A. and T.

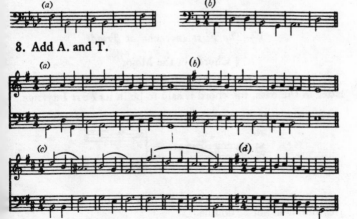

9. Harmonize the following melodies in four parts:

1 chord   1 chord

V—The First Inversion of Triads

$\frac{6}{3}$ Chords in the Major

1. If the root of a chord be placed above the 3rd, leaving the latter in the bass, the chord is said to be in its *First Inversion*.

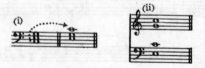

In (ii) the note C is still the *root* of the chord; E is the Major 3rd, and must not be doubled.

2. *Figuring of chords.*

3. A $\frac{6}{3}$ chord may be formed on each degree of a Major scale.

Note—

(i) In minor triads there is no objection to doubling the 3rd: in a *diminished* triad the 3rd should, as a rule, be doubled.

(ii) With the exception of viiºb it may be said that a chord in its first inversion is weaker than the same chord in its root-position.

(iii) All chords of the Major Diatonic scale are now available in the first inversion.

4. *Use of $\frac{6}{3}$ chords.*

(i) Following the *same* chord in its Root-position.

(ii) Following a $\frac{5}{3}$ on the same Bass note, strong to weak.

(iii) With the Bass moving a step to or from the $\frac{6}{3}$ chord.

(Note the doubling of the Bass note in vii°*b*.)
    (iv) With the Bass descending a 3rd from another $\frac{5}{3}$ or
        chord.

(v) In a succession of $\frac{6}{3}$ chords with the Bass moving scale
wise upwards or downwards*.

* This is the only way in which iii*b* may be used for the present.

In this case, except for the second chord of ex. (a), the Soprano moves in consecutive 6ths with the Bass, the Alto in consecutive 3rds, and the Tenor in alternate 3rds and 6ths.

5. Progressions such as v—IV, ii—I, which were not available in root-position, can now be used with the chords in first inversion.

iib   Ib

6. Note the various ways in which vii°b may be used.

(a) *Between* I *and* Ib.   (b) *Between* IV *and* I.   (c) *Between* IV *and* vi.

viib   viib   viib   viib

A *Perfect 5th* may be followed by a *Diminished 5th* (and *vice versa*) between two upper parts* provided the *lower* of the two moves *by step of a semitone*.

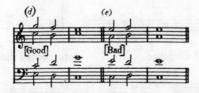

In (e) the lower of the two parts proceeding in fifths (the Alto) does not keep the rule.

* *Two upper parts,* i.e., any two parts not including the Bass.

117

Never use vii°b to precede the Dominant; V—vii°b may b
used, but only from strong to weak.

V — vii°b

7. iib may be used as a decoration of the Subdominan
chord and over the same Bass note; vib may also be used simi
larly as a decoration of the Tonic chord. .

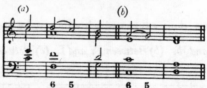

8. The Bass of a Primary chord ($\frac{5}{3}$ or $\frac{6}{3}$) will generally b
free to leap to another Primary chord ($\frac{5}{3}$ or $\frac{6}{3}$), but it will b
advisable for the present to use root-position chords when th
Bass leaps a Perfect 4th or 5th.

9. $\frac{6}{3}$ chords can be used to *approach* a Cadence:

Perfect Cadence.   Imperfect Cadence.

Plagal Cadence.   Interrupted Cadence.

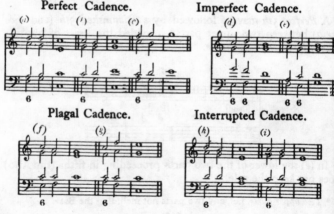

EXERCISES

1. Add parts S.A.T. making $\frac{6}{3}$ chords.

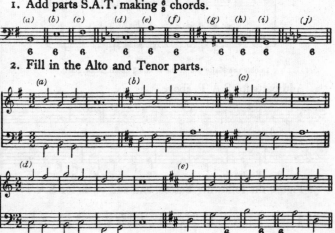

2. Fill in the Alto and Tenor parts.

3. Write $\frac{6}{3}$ chords instead of those marked*; change the chord if necessary but do not change the melody.

I

Double the Major 3rd in the second ⁶₄ chord (scalic Bass).

4. Add parts for S.A.T. above.

5. Figure the following Basses, and add parts for S.A.T.

6. Harmonize for S.A.T.B.

$^6_3$ Chords of a Minor Key

1. The first inversions of the chords of a minor key (harmonic form) are as follows:

i(b) ii°b iv(b) V(b) VI(b) vii°b   IIIb

Under the present limitations the Chord III^1 b cannot be used*. Notice that ii°b and vii°b are the inversions of *Diminished* triads.

2. First inversions may be used in a minor key as in the major; care should be taken with regard to intervals of the Augmented 2nd and the Augmented 4th which occur diatonically in the Harmonic Minor Scale.

The use of the chords will be as follows:

(i) Instead of the same chord $^5_3$.

(ii) Following a $^5_3$ on the same Bass note.

(iii) Decorating a $^5_3$ on the same Bass note.

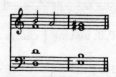

* See page 149 for explanation of notation.

(iv) With the Bass moving a step to or from a $\frac{5}{3}$.

(v) With the Bass descending a 3rd from a $\frac{5}{3}$ or $\frac{6}{3}$.

(vi) In a succession of $\frac{6}{3}$ chords with the Bass moving scalewi‹
upwards or downwards.

* The *Minor* 7th of the scale in a descending passage.

EXERCISES

1. Write one chord to precede, and one to follow each of th
following:

2. Add parts for A.T.B. making $\frac{6}{3}$ chords:

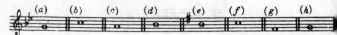

3. Fill in A. and T. parts in the following:

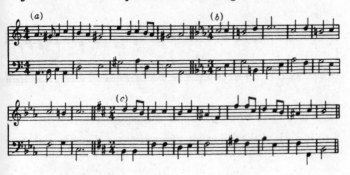

4. Add parts for S.A.T.

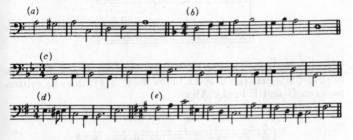

5. Add parts for A.T.B.

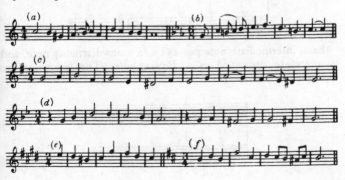

6. Add ⁶₃ chords in the spaces marked *.

VI—Unaccented Passing-notes

1. In each of the following progressions a diatonic note may be written between consecutive harmony notes a third apart.

In (a) the note D may be written between E and C in the Soprano, and between C and E in the Bass; in (b) F may be written between G and E in the Alto.

Each intermediate note passes on to a new harmony note, and is therefore described as a *Passing-note*. The following are examples in a minor key:

2. Two parts may use passing-notes together. In this case, the parts must move in parallel 3rds or 6ths, or take the same passing-note in contrary motion.

(a) Parallel 3rds.

(b) Parallel 6ths.

(c) Same note taken in contrary motion.

 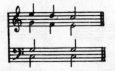 

3. *Considerations affecting Passing-notes.*

(i) The Perfect 4th from the root of a chord cannot be used as a *descending* passing-note with the 3rd still sounding.

The bad effect may be avoided by taking *two* passing-notes together as in par. 2 above.

(ii) A passing-note must not produce consecutive fifths or octaves.

(iii) *Passing-notes do not remove the effect of consecutive fifths or octaves.* A progression which would be incorrect without a passing-note is equally incorrect with it.

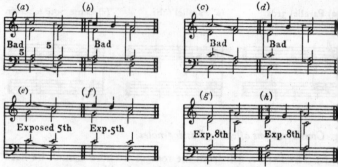

(iv) A passing-note should not run *into* a chord note (2 into 1)

Or cause a 2nd between it and a chord note to be quitted by *similar* motion.

(v) If the 2nd or 4th from the root of a chord be used as a passing-note, no harmony note should be struck with it.

In (b) the passing-note is struck immediately *after* the chord note.

4. *Two passing-notes may be taken in succession over* I*a* or IV*a* in the major, and i*a* or VI*a* in the minor. They should be used from the 5th to the root of the chord (ascending) and from the root to the 5th (descending). No notes should be struck *with* the passing-notes for the present.

5. A chord note may be struck with the 7th from the root used as a passing-note; similarly the 6th and the root may be struck together.

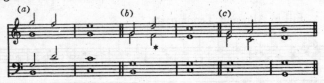

6. The Minor 7th of the scale may be used as a passing-note (ascending or descending) over chords iv and VI in a minor key.

7. The Major 6th of the Melodic minor scale is used as a passing-note as follows:

a) Ascending or descending over **V**

(*b*) Ascending over **I**

EXERCISES

1. Add passing-notes:

2. Fill in Alto and Tenor parts.

3. Harmonize for S.A.T.B.

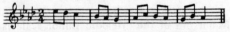

4. Add parts for S.A.T. above the following:

128

1. The *Second Inversion* of a chord has the 5th in the **Bass**—the root and the 3rd being placed above it.

I   I (c)

2. It is figured $^6_4$ thus:

3. It may be treated under the following headings:

(a) *Cadential* $^6_4$. This is used *on the accent*, over the Tonic or Dominant of the scale: it resolves $^6_4$—$^5_3$ on the same Bass note.

Three points to be memorized:

> (i) The note to double is the Bass, i.e. the *5th* of the chord.
>
> (ii) The Bass note remains whilst the chord resolves.
>
> (iii) The 6th must fall to the 5th and the 4th to the 3rd.

Approach to a Cadential $\frac{6}{4}$.

A Cadential $\frac{6}{4}$ cannot be approached by leap from an inversion of another chord. It may be approached from another position of the *same* chord, or by step in the Bass from an available $\frac{5}{3}$ or $\frac{6}{3}$ chord, or by leap of a Perfect 4th upwards (or 5th downwards) from another $\frac{5}{3}$ chord*.

Each of the above $\frac{6}{4}$—$\frac{5}{3}$ progressions is really a decoration of the $\frac{5}{3}$ chord upon which the $\frac{6}{4}$ resolves; example (a) is really an ornamented form of:

A Cadential $\frac{6}{4}$ is used on the first or third beat of a bar in Common time, or the first or second beat in Triple time; these are strong, or relatively strong accents.

* Except ii° in the minor.

130

The following are examples of Cadential $_4^6$ chords in a minor key:

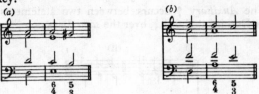

(b) *A Passing* $_4^6$ is used on a weak accent between I*a* and I*b* or *vice versa*, or between IV*a* and IV*b* and *vice versa*.

The $_4^6$ between I*a* and I*b* should be compared with a $_8^6$ used similarly; we have now three ways of harmonizing the same melodic phrase.

Choice of chord must depend upon the context, but (*b*) is generally to be preferred to (*a*)

(c) The *Arpeggio* $_4^6$ is approached from the root-position or the first inversion of the same chord.

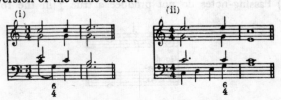

The Bass must proceed to another position of the same chord, as in (i), or by step to another $\frac{5}{3}$ or $\frac{6}{3}$ chord, as in (ii).

(d) The *Auxiliary* $\frac{6}{4}$ occurs between two statements of the Tonic or Dominant chord $\frac{5}{3}$, over the *same* Bass note.

4. *Observations on $\frac{6}{4}$ chords.*

(a) A $\frac{6}{4}$ chord on a strong accent should be resolved $\frac{6}{4}$—$\frac{5}{3}$ on the same Bass note:

(b) A $\frac{6}{4}$ should not be used for the *first* position of a chord.

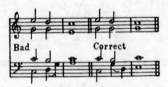

(c) Passing-notes do not produce a true $\frac{6}{4}$ in the following case.

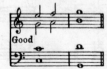

The above is satisfactory provided that *both* passing-notes proceed onwards to a new chord note. In the example below, the F in the Soprano does not pass onwards *with* the Alto and produces an unresolved $^6_4$.

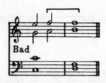

Bad

EXERCISES

1. Resolve the following chords as Cadential $^6_4$ chords. Show *two* ways of approaching each one.

(a)

(i)   (ii)   (iii)   (iv)

(b)

(i)   (ii)   (iii)   (iv)

2. Harmonize the following for S.A.T.B.:

(a)
I IV Ic V I

(b)
I iib Ic V I

(c)
Ib vi Ic V I

(d)
i iib⁰ iv ic V i

(e)
I Ib Ic V I

(f)
I vi iib Ic V I

(g)
V ib i ic V i

133

3. Harmonize for S.A.T.B.:

4. Add A.T.B.:

5. Write Passing $^6_4$ chords at the points marked *:

6. Add Auxiliary $^6_4$ chords at *:

7. (a) Introduce an Arpeggio $^6_4$ into each of the following:

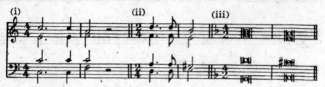

(b) Explain:

$^6_4 = {}^{\#6}_4$

8. Add parts for A. and T.:

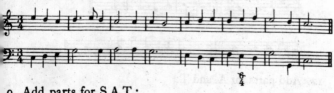

9. Add parts for S.A.T.:

10. Add parts for S.A.T.:

(a)

(b)

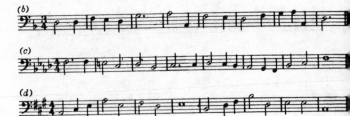

(c)

(d)

11. Harmonize for S.A.T.B.:

(a)

(b)

(c)

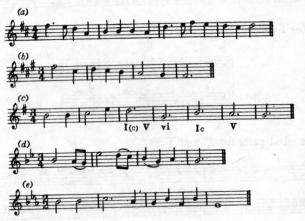

I(c) V   vi   Ic   V

(d)

(e)

12. Add parts for A. and T.:

13. Harmonize:

VIII—Accented Passing Notes

1. A passing-note may be struck simultaneously with the chord into which it passes. It is then called an *Accented passing-note*, and must be approached and quitted by step.

In (i) F is an *accented* passing-note, in (ii) it is *unaccented*.

2. The following points should be mastered.

(*a*) An accented passing-note may not be struck against its note of resolution except:

(i) when the note of resolution is in the Bass,

or (ii) when the note of resolution is approached by step and in contrary motion to that of the passing-note.

(b) Accented passing-notes are generally better *descending* than ascending, but *parallel* ascending passing-notes may be used freely—one note passing between the root and the third of a chord, and the other between the third and the fifth.

(c) Two parts may take the same passing-note by contrary motion between the root and third of a chord, or between the third and fifth.

EXERCISES

1. Add accented passing-notes:

2. Add parts for A. and T.:

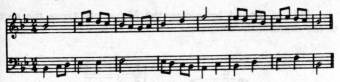

3. Harmonize for S.A.T.B.:

(a)

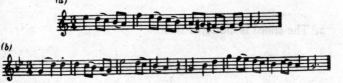

(b)

4. Add parts for S.A.T., using accented passing-notes where possible:

(a)

(b)

5. Add three vocal parts below the following melody for Soprano voice:

Irish melody.

6. Add three vocal parts above the following Bass part; write in open score, and with C clef for Alto and Tenor parts *Andante*:

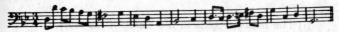

IX—The Dominant Seventh

1. This is formed by adding the Minor 7th above the root to the chord of the Dominant.

2. The chord is indicated thus:

3. The Seventh being a discord must not be doubled.

4. *Resolution of the Dominant Seventh.*
(A) *First resolution (V⁷—Ia).*

(i) The Bass proceeds to the Tonic of the scale.
(ii) The Seventh falls a semitone.

(iii) The Leading-note rises a semitone*.

Note that in the progression V⁷—Ia (in four parts, both chords in root-position) *one* of the chords will have its fifth omitted.

In resolving a V⁷, no two parts may proceed in consecutive intervals of a Seventh and an Octave (7–8).

(B) *Second Resolution* (V⁷–via).

V7 - via

The Bass rises a step but otherwise the chord resolves as before—the Seventh falling and the Third rising a step.

In a minor key the progression is written:

Notice that the Major 3rd of the Submediant chord *has to be doubled* to make a correct progression.

* In a cadence, the Leading-note when occurring in a middle part may *fall* to the fifth of the final chord in order to have the last chord in complete form.

BACH. ' St Matthew Passion.'

(c) *Resolution on the Subdominant.*

V^7 IV_b V^7_b V^7_b IV_c I

Here, the Seventh remains to be a part of the succeeding chord. In (i) the Subdominant occurs between two positions of the Dominant 7th, with the Bass passing by step; in (ii) the Subdominant merely delays the resolution of the Dominant 7th on to Tonic harmony.

5. *Inversions of the Dominant Seventh.*

The following are the three inversions of the Dominant Seventh with their figuration:

The Seventh resolves downwards and the Leading-note upwards as before.

(a)   (b)   (c)

6. *Approach to the Dominant Seventh.*

(a)   (b)

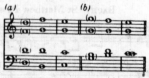

(i) In its *root-position* and *first inversion* the chord may be approached as if it were an ordinary V*a* or V*b*.

142

(ii) In its *second inversion* it will generally be approached from
I*b* or from another position of V or V⁷.

But note the following as a decoration of the strong progression
IV—I.

(iii) *The Dominant 7th in its last (third) inversion* may be
approached from any of the ⁵₃ or ⁶₃ chords at present available
excepting vii° and possibly vi.

(Choice of chord must be left to individual discretion.)

A leap of a Minor 7th upwards from the Dominant Common
chord (⁵₃) is good.

The *same* bass note may be used from weak to strong thus:

(iv) In the progression vi—V⁷d, care must be taken to avoid approaching a Ninth by similar motion; a *Seventh* by similar motion is generally allowed.

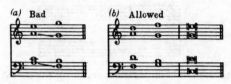

(v) A V⁷d may be used to follow the second inversion of the Tonic chord:

7. *Other Resolutions of the Dominant Seventh.*

(i) A *Seventh may rise* if the Bass moves upwards in parallel thirds with it.

(ii) A Seventh may proceed to the note above, or below its note of resolution before resolving.

(iii) It may leap to another note of the same chord—the resolution being effected through another part.

Except in the Bass, where it should resolve if it once gets there.

(iv) In the following a *transitory* Seventh in the highest part doubles the Seventh in the Bass and then proceeds upwards.

This is allowable in a very quick passage.

EXERCISES

1. Resolve each of the following into the Tonic chord:

2. Write the following chords for S.A.T.B. and resolve them into the Tonic chord:

3. Resolve into the Submediant chord:

145

4. Resolve:

5. Write the following chords for S.A.T.B. and resolve them:

6. In each of the spaces * write a chord which resolves the preceding V⁷:

7. Add parts for A. and T.:

8. Add parts for A.T.B.:

9. Add parts for S.A.T.:

(c) Unfigured

(d)

(e)

10. Harmonize for S.A.T.B.:

(a)

(b)

(c) Andante

(d)

(e)

(f)

I   (vi)

148

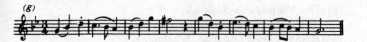

X.—*vii°a in the Major and Minor. ii°a in the Minor. The Mediant in the Major and Minor*

(A) *Diminished and Augmented triads in root-position.*

1. The following are discords, and should be used sparingly:

The Leading-note (major and minor keys) and the Supertonic (minor keys only) are *Diminished* triads, whilst the Mediant of a minor key is an *Augmented* triad. The notation for an Augmented triad is a large Roman numeral with a dash (') as shown.

2. When using these chords, the fifth must be prepared by writing it in the same voice-part in the preceding chord.

The Diminished 5th from the Bass resolves downwards a semitone; the Augmented 5th *rises* a semitone into the chord a Perfect 4th above.

3. The *fifth* should not be doubled in either a Diminished or an Augmented triad.

(B) *The Mediant in a Major Key.*

1. iii*a* in the Major should be preceded and followed by a chor
containing at least one note in common.

When harmonizing a downward scale it may be followed by IV*a*

Note the progression I—iii*a* (*weak* to *strong*, roots *rising*
third), which is allowed in this particular case.

2. iii*b* in the Major.

The first inversion of the Mediant may be used in *two* ways
(*a*) As a *true* Mediant (iii*b*).
(*b*) As a decoration of the Dominant (V).

Used as a true Mediant it must be approached and quitted b
step in the Bass, or by a leap in the Bass from the same chord $\frac{5}{3}$.

Note that the *Leading-note may be doubled* in the chord of the
Mediant as in (*b*) above.

The following are examples of iii*b* used as a decoration of the Dominant chord:

In (*a*) and (*b*) the Sixth from the Bass resolves one step downwards; in (*c*) the Sixth falls a Third into a new chord.

The Seventh from the Bass may be added *provided* it is sounded below the Sixth.

It will be noticed that (*a*) and (*b*) have the effect of *Full* Closes; while (*c*) and (*d*) effect *False* Closes.

(c) III′*b* *in the minor* is used as a decoration (or instead of) the Dominant. The Seventh from the Bass may be added as in the major provided it is sounded below the Sixth.

The exposed octaves in (*b*) and (*c*) are allowed.

The Minor 6th from the Bass (E♭) may be *enharmonically changed* to D♯ and the chord then resolved as an Augmented triad on the Dominant of the major key.

EXERCISES

1. Add parts for A. and T.:

2. Prepare and resolve each of the following chords:

3. Harmonize the following, using the resource mentioned above:

4. Add parts for A. and T.:

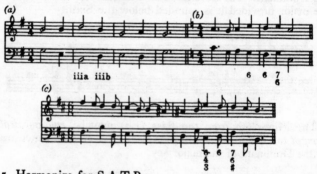

5. Harmonize for S.A.T.B.:

(b)

6. Add parts for A. and T.:

* Subdominant chord with **sharpened third**.

7. Add three vocal parts above:

(a)

(b)

(c)

* *vb* of descending Melodic minor scale.

8. Add A. and T.:

(a)

(t)

9. Add A. and T.:

XI—Suspensions

1. In the following example:

a note of the first chord is held over into the second, afterwards being allowed to fall and become a part of the latter. The note held over is called a *suspension*, and its occurrence in the same part in the preceding chord constitutes its *preparation*. When the suspended note becomes part of the chord over which it has been suspended it is said to be *resolved*.

Examples:

Note also:

2. Each of the above suspensions is named by the figures which are placed underneath it; these indicate the interval which the suspended note and its resolution make with the Bass.

Notice that only *one* rising suspension is given for the present, viz., with the Leading-note rising to the Tonic over the chord of the Tonic.

3. In a suspension the discord must occur on a *strong* accent and resolve on a weak. The duration of the *preparation* should not be less than (and will generally be equal to) that of the discord.

4. A suspended note may not be sounded *with* its note of resolution except:

(i) when the note of resolution is in the Bass:

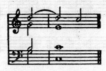

or (ii) when the part containing the note of resolution proceeds by step *and* in contrary motion to that of the suspended note:

5. The following progressions contain consecutive fifths and octaves, and are faulty:

6. A note of suspension may proceed to the note next above it, or to the note a step below the resolution, or to a chord note, before finally resolving:

1. Rewrite the following, introducing suspensions:

2. Add parts for A. and T.:

3. Rewrite the following without suspensions:

4. Add A. and T.:

5. Add S. and T.:

6. Harmonize for S.A.T.B.:

7. Add S.A.T.:

8. Add two melodious parts below the given violin part; write in short score:

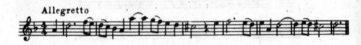

XII—Modulation

1. In the course of a movement a piece of music generally passes out of one key and into another; this process is called Modulation.

2. A new key is established by the progression V—I in that key provided that one of the chords in the progression contains a note foreign to the key quitted*.

In (a) the last chord but one contains F♯, which is foreign to the key quitted (C major); the progression V—I in G major therefore establishes the new key. The second example (b) ends with a Full Close in F major but does not modulate because there is no note which is foreign to the key of C major.

* It may also be established by a ' False Close ' (V—VI) in the new key; or even by the ⁶₄ of the new Tonic.

3. *Use of a Pivot Chord.*

Modulation may be effected by means of a Pivot chord, i.e., one which belongs to the key quitted and also to the new key, and not generally being the Tonic of the first key, or the Tonic or Dominant of the second. Thus A minor would be a Pivot chord between C major and G major.

The Pivot chord is approached in the first key and quitted in the second, which is then established by means of a Full Close.

If the Full Close in the new key does not introduce a note foreign to the key quitted this may be done by means of a chord belonging to the new key—immediately after the Pivot.

Or the Minor 7th may be added to the Dominant.

4. Modulation may take place to a *nearly related* key, or to a *remote* key; the Tonic, Dominant, and Subdominant with their relatives are classed as nearly related keys.

Table of Modulations to nearly related keys

To the:	Example	Pivot Chord
Relative Minor	C major to A minor	F major; D minor
Relative Major	A minor to C major	B diminished
Dominant	C major to G major	A minor; E minor
	A minor to E minor	A minor
Subdominant	C major to F major	A minor; D minor
	A minor to D minor	D minor
Supertonic Minor	C major to D minor	D minor
Mediant Minor	C major to E minor	A minor
Relative Major of Dominant	A minor to G major	A minor
Relative Major of Subdominant	A minor to F major	D minor

Examples:

(i) C major to G major

(ii) A minor to E minor

(iii) A minor to C major

(iv) C major to A minor

(v) A minor to D minor

(vi) C major to D minor

(vii) C major to E minor

vi
iv

[V — i]

5. Observations on Modulation.

(i) Avoid having two forms of the same chord (major and minor) with only one other chord between them.

Bad

Even when two chords intervene, the G and the G♯ should not appear in the same part, especially if this be the melody.

(a) Bad

(b) Amend thus

(ii) A note which is foreign to the key quitted must not be used as a diatonic passing-note until it has been heard as an essential note.

) Bad

(b) Good

(iii) If *two* modulations occur in a phrase the *first* new key should be established with its Tonic chord in the first inversion, or by means of a V—VI progression in that key; the *second* key may then be established by a Full Close at the end of the phrase.

(iv) It will sometimes become necessary to use the Tonic of the first or the second key as a Pivot chord (*vide* examples of modulation given above from a minor key to its Dominant and from a major key to its Supertonic minor).

XIII—*Modulation without a Pivot Chord*

1. A change of key may be effected without a Pivot chord, and is then called a *Transition* or *abrupt modulation*.

In each of these cases, the chord which introduces the note foreign to the key quitted contains a note in common with the preceding chord.

2. A transition should not occur at the *end* of a phrase; but it will often be useful at the beginning of a phrase (excepting the first), or in the course of a phrase.

3. In a Transition, the note which is chromatically altered (sharpened or flattened) must be kept in the *same* part.

The bad effect in the above examples is termed ' *false relation* ': it is felt even with a chord intervening.

4. False relation is not produced in the following cases:

    (i) When a Minor 3rd is sharpened in a cadence producing a *Tierce de Picardie.*

    (ii) When the Minor 7th of the Melodic Minor Scale (descending) is used as a harmony note.

    (iii) When the Major 3rd of a chord is flattened and becomes the seventh of another chord, e.g., V⁷.

5. False relation is not generally produced when the third of one chord remains to become the *root* or *fifth* of the succeeding chord, or *vice versa.*

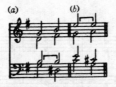

This is a matter for the sensitive ear to decide; for the present a note chromatically altered should be kept in the *same* part.

6. *Use of Sequence.*

A harmonic or melodic progression may be repeated immediately at a higher or lower pitch, making a *Sequence.*

It will be noticed that (*b*) is an exact reproduction of (*a*) with all the notes a semitone lower. All the intervals found in the first two chords are reproduced in (*b*)—this makes a *Real Sequence.*

When the intervals in the first progression are *not* reproduced exactly a *Tonal Sequence* results.

A *Real Sequence* produces modulation from one major key to another, or from one minor key to another.

A *Tonal Sequence* may produce modulation from a major to a minor key (or *vice versa*), or possibly not effect any modulation at all.

Tonal Sequence.

7. In using a sequence to effect change of key the procedure will be as follows:

Example: To modulate from D major to C major commencing thus:

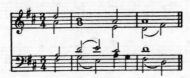

(*a*) The sequence must be ' *real* ' because there is no change of mode from D major to C major.

(*b*) Transposition must be *downwards* a tone.

(*c*) The first chord I*b* in D major, when transposed, must make a good *join* with the last chord (I*a*) of the given phrase.

When transposed the first chord of the exercise becomes the chord of C major ⁶₃; this makes a good progression with the chord of D ⁵₃; the sequence is therefore effected as follows:

Transposed:

Giving:

The next case shows the use of a *Tonal Sequence*.
Modulation from C major to A minor.

From this exercise two points have emerged:

    (i) The progression V—vi establishes a key, although
        does not actually confirm it.

    (ii) A chord may be repeated from weak to strong at th
        beginning of a new phrase.

EXERCISES

1. The following is a modulation from C major to G majo
using the pivot chord A minor:

Proceeding similarly, complete the following phrases b
adding a further two bars, modulating to the Dominant, th
Subdominant, the Relative Major or Minor in each case.

(c)

2. To the following phrases add one or two bars completing the modulations:

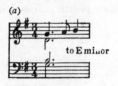

(a) to E minor

(b) to B♭ major

3. Modulate:

to the Mediant minor   to the Subdominant

4. Harmonize for S.A.T.B., modulating as shown:

(a) C maj.   G maj.   *(b)* G maj. E min. ——— C maj.

(c) D maj.   A maj.

5. Repeat the following chord-progressions *in sequence* so as to modulate as indicated:

(a) to A minor

(b) to C minor

6. Example:

Proceeding as above, repeat each of the following phrases in sequence, modulating to the given key, then return and end in the original key.

(a) to G major

(b) to E minor

(c) to E major

(d) to Dᵇ major

7. Add parts for S.A.T.:

C major

A minor and G major

C and F major

C major

8.

(a) Write a five-bar phrase in Simple-Triple time, modulating from D major to B minor. Four-part harmony is to be used.

(b) Write a three-bar phrase in Quadruple time, modulating from F major to A minor. Use short score.

9. Add S.A.T. parts to the following figured Bass. Write in open score and use C clefs for the Alto and Tenor parts:

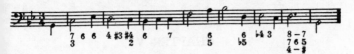

10. Add three vocal parts to the following figured Bass:

CHAPTER V

THREE-PART WRITING

1. Generally speaking, it will be well to make the parts inde
pendent and to distribute them equally: a wide gap should onl
occur between the two lowest parts.

BEETHOVEN. Trio in G major, Op. 9, No. 1.

If a fifth or octave, occurring between *any* two parts, be ap
proached by similar motion between different chords, the uppe
part forming the interval should move by step:

2. *Passing-notes*. Care should be taken that two passing-notes
which have *begun* to proceed together in thirds or sixths continue
to do so until they arrive at chord notes *together*.

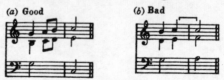

3. The second or fourth from the root (used as a passing-note) should not be struck with a chord note except between two statements of the same chord as in (a):

When used between two different chords, the second or fourth (as a passing-note) should be struck *after* the chord note, as in (c).

4. The Seventh from the root may be struck with any note of a chord provided it then resolves; the Sixth as a passing-note may be sounded with the *root*.

5. Auxiliary notes* may be used in combination, producing a passing chord between two statements of the same harmony.

6. When two or more notes of short duration can be harmonized by one long note it is necessary to decide which is to be the harmony note. Choose the one which effects the better progression.

* See page 87.

The progression V—IV obtained by harmonizing the **first of** the two short notes (as in the second example) is weak **compared** with the implied progression V—I*b* in the first.

7. *Examples.*
   (i) Melody given: two parts added.

   (ii) Lowest part given:

   (iii) Three-part String Writing:

BEETHOVEN. Trio in E flat, Op. 3.

The aim should be to produce a consistent figuration in **each** part as in (iii), or to have one central figure or idea **worked** through the whole as in (ii).

8. *Pianoforte Writing.*

Three-part work forms a convenient point of approach to pianoforte writing: advantage should be taken of the following points of procedure:

(A) (i) The Bass may be doubled freely at the octave below.

SCHUMANN. 'Album for the Young', No. 29.

HAYDN. Pianoforte Sonata in C.

(*a*)

(*b*)

(*Bass in broken octaves*)

(ii) An upper or middle part may be doubled.

BEETHOVEN. Pianoforte Sonata in F Minor, Op. 2, No. 1.
(*c*)

GRIEG. 'Poetische Tonbilder.'
(*d*)

But consecutives should not occur between an upper or middle part and the Bass.

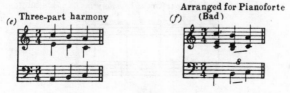

(*e*) Three-part harmony

Arranged for Pianoforte
(*f*) (Bad)

173

(iii) A Major 3rd, or a discord, or the Leading-note of a scale may be doubled in an upper part, provided that it does not already occur in the bass.

SCHUBERT. Impromptu, Op. 142, No. 2.

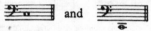

(iv) As a working rule, it may be taken that notes written between

should be more than a third apart. Those below:

will usually be an octave apart.

(v) Care must be taken not to write combinations of notes which the hands cannot play. In the following, (a) involves too great a span for the fingers and must be rearranged.

The use of the sustaining pedal, as in (b), makes wide spans possible in the left hand.

(B) *Arrangement of chords in arpeggiated or detached forms.*

174

(i) It will be noticed that the effect of the real bass in such combinations persists until another note is heard in the same register. The following would be bad:

The effect at both (a) and (b) is that of two chords sounding together, and is therefore unpleasant.

(ii) The harmony may be amplified by doubling the bass or an upper part, and then arranging the chords as for pianoforte.

(a) *Bass doubled.*   (b) *Upper part doubled.*

Arranged as for pianoforte.

(c)    (d)

(iii) The correctness of the harmony in such passages may be tested by writing the chords in unbroken form.

(a)  = (b)

(c) *Pianoforte Accompaniment.*

(i) An upper part of the accompaniment may duplicate the solo temporarily at the unison or the octave: the bass should not be allowed to do so.

BEETHOVEN. ' An die Geliebte.'

O dass ich dir vom st:l-len Au-ge

pp

(ii) Consecutive fifths and octaves must not occur between the bass and the solo part; and no upper part of the accompaniment should double the bass*.

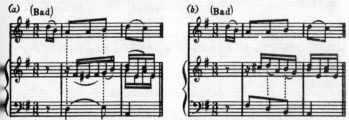

(iii) The accompaniment should be complete in itself, but may consist only of a single part. The Leading-note of the scale, the Major 3rd, or a discord belonging to the solo part may be reproduced as a factor of the accompaniment.

(iv) The accompaniment should usually have some definite figuration, maintained with a degree of consistency; any variation of figure should generally occur at, or towards, the cadences.

* Unless the passage be entirely in octaves.

BEETHOVEN. ' Mit einem gemalten Band.'

Kleine Blumen, kleine Blätter etc.

SCHUBERT. Violin Sonata in C.

EXERCISES

1. Add an inner part to the following:

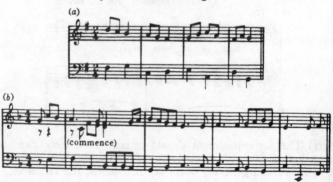

2. Write two parts below the following melody:

3. To the melodies for first violin given below, add parts for violin and violoncello:

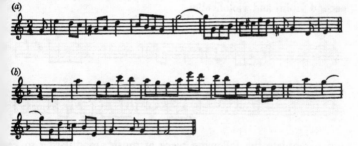

(a)

(b)

4. Add Tenor and Bass parts to this melody. Do not use more than two chords a bar.

(a)

5. Continue this Trio, writing as for Violin, Viola, and 'Cello

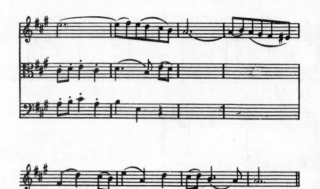

6. To the melody given below, add parts in open score for second violin and violoncello:

7. Complete the following piece of music, modulating to E♭ major. Write for Treble, Alto and Bass:

Describe the chord marked with an asterisk.

8. Write a simple piano piece, beginning as follows, modulating through D major, B minor, A minor, G major (about sixteen bars in all).

9. To the melody for first violin given below, add parts in open score for second violin and violoncello.

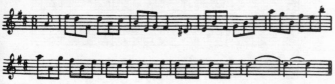

Pianoforte Writing.

10. Arrange each of the following chords and progressions in three ways, writing for pianoforte; vary the density of the harmony in each case.

11. Rearrange the following in various ways, suitable for pianoforte.

12. Arrange the following vocal harmony for pianoforte, double the Bass and upper parts where necessary.

MENDELSSOHN. 'Lift thine Eyes'

13. Harmonize the following for pianoforte, continuing as indicated in the first two bars:

14. (*a*) Using the given harmony, rewrite the accompaniment to the following, commencing as shown:

(Melody and harmony by BEETHOVEN.)

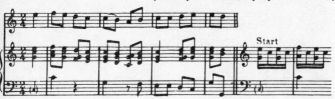

(*b*) Add an accompaniment to the following melody, commencing as shown:

(*b*)

15. Write a pianoforte accompaniment to each of the following melodies:

(*a*)

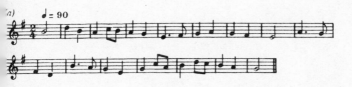

(b) Andante

(c) Andante ♩ = 80

(d)

Accompaniments should also be written to the melodies given in questions 3(*a*) and (*b*), 6 and 9.

CHAPTER VI

FORM

A piece of music will generally be found to divide itself into clearly defined rhythmic periods which indicate the plan or structural mode of arrangement of the material. This constitutes the form of the music, or the means by which unity and proportion are attained.

For convenience it is necessary to classify the larger rhythmic periods into *Sentences* and *Phrases*. A phrase is only a partial statement consisting of two or more (usually four) strong accents, and ending with some form of cadence : it requires to be followed by another similar statement to produce a satisfactory feeling of balance.   BEETHOVEN. Pianoforte Sonata, Op. 2, No. 2.

A *sentence* is a period consisting of two or more phrases, ending usually with a Full Close.*

* The phrases frequently subdivide into *sections* and *motives*.

The following is a sentence containing three phrases:

Phrases labeled: A [Half Close], B [False Close], C [Full Close]

Binary Form*.

In essentials, a Binary form consists of two complementary sentences—the first modulating *away* from the Tonic (e.g., to the Dominant or the Relative major) and the second taking the music back to a Full Close in the home key†.

CORELLI. ' Sonata da Camera a tre.'

[A major]

[D major]

Frequently, it will be found that the same idea occurs in complementary keys at the beginning of the first and second half. Thus in Handel's ' Fantasia for harpsichord ' in C major, the first half commences thus:

* See also p. 70, par. 16, ' *Melodies in Binary Form* '.

† It is not absolutely essential that change of key should take place (*vide* the Andante of Beethoven's Pianoforte Sonata in F minor, Op. 57, and the song ' Morgen steh' ich auf und frage ' (SCHUMANN, Op. 24, No. 1).

The *second half* commences with the same idea in the Dominant and leads back to the Tonic.

Frequently, too, the *after-phrase* of the first half will reappear as the end of the second half, transposed so as to lead back to the home key instead of away from it as in the first half. (*Vide* the *Courante* of Handel's Fourth Suite, and that of Bach's Fifth French Suite.)

Simple Ternary Form.

This consists of a leading statement A, followed by a contrasting section B, leading to a return of the opening section A, ending in the Tonic.

The sections are frequently given to be repeated so as to conform with the following plan:

$$A : \| : B A : \|$$

HAYDN. String Quartet, Op. 3, No. 3.

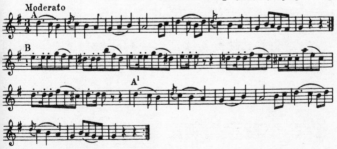

A more extended example is to be found in the *Andante* of Beethoven's Sonata in G major, Op. 79.

Examples of the form are frequently to be found in folk-songs, e.g., 'The Bluebells of Scotland', 'The Jolly Miller', and 'All through the Night' (see page 71).

187

Minuet and Trio Form*.

In the sonatas, etc., of Haydn and Mozart, each movement of the Minuet and Trio makes a complete Binary or Ternary form, usually with distinct contrast of idea and of key. In performance the movements are played in the order:

MINUET	TRIO	MINUET†
A : ‖ : BA¹: ‖	a : ‖ : ba¹ : ‖	A ‖ BA¹ ‖

making a Ternary order of *movements*, the Minuet corresponding to the opening statement A of a Simple Ternary form, the Trio to the digression B, and the Minuet repeated to the restatement A¹.

The following illustrates the character of a Haydn Minuet:

HAYDN. Quartet, Op. 55, No. 1

Trio begins:

* In the early Suites, two minuets frequently occur in immediate succession: Minuet I and Minuet II. In course of time the second Minuet came to be played by a trio of instruments, and hence to be known as the Trio; the movements were played in the order: Minuet, Trio, Minuet.

† Note that the *sections* of the Minuet are not usually repeated in the restatement.

Originally the Minuet was a slow and rather stately dance in triple time ($\frac{3}{4}$ or $\frac{3}{8}$), and commencing invariably with the *first* beat of the bar.

BACH. Minuet from French Suite, No. IV.

By commencing with the *third* beat instead of the first, and prescribing a somewhat quicker tempo, Haydn gave to the dance a much lighter and livelier character*.

Later, the place of the Minuet and Trio came to be taken by the Scherzo and Trio—each movement having the same plan as the Minuet, but endowed with a livelier, more jocund character.

THE SIMPLE RONDO

The Rondo seems to have had its origin in a common type of song, a part of which was made to recur by singing it over and over again, with solo portions in between. The practice, it is said, was for a band of minstrels to begin by singing the chorus together, and for one of them to continue with a solo portion: the rest would then join in with the same chorus as before, and the whole process repeated at length until finally all joined with the chorus to finish.

Another possibility is that it was a dance ' the music to which was sung whilst the performers danced in a circle. . . . It began with a chorus; one of the dancers then sang a solo, after which the chorus was repeated as a refrain. Other solos followed, the chorus being repeated after each. The chorus itself was called the " Rondeau ", and the various solos " Couplets "†.'

* With Mozart, both forms are almost equally common; not more than one in four of Beethoven's minuets commences on the first beat.

† Prout, *Applied Forms.*

A Rondo then consists of a central, recurrent musical idea, i which interest is maintained by means of 'episodes', or contrastin portions, heard between the several repetitions of the main theme The form may be related to that of a verse Rondel such as t following:

> The year has cast its wede away
>> Of rain, of tempest and of cold,
>> And put on broidery of gold
> Of sunbeams bright and clear and gay. } A
> There is no bird or beast to-day
>> But sings and shouts in field and fold, } B
> ' The year has cast its wede away
>> Of rain, of tempest and of cold'. } A¹

> The silver fret-work of the May
>> Is over brook and spring enscrolled,
>> A blazon lovely to behold. } C
> Each thing has put on new array:
> The year has cast its wede away
>> Of rain, of tempest and of cold. } A"

(C. d'Orleans, *Le temps a laissé*. Trans. by J. Payne.*

The works of Couperin provide excellent examples of the earl rondo form. A principal theme (called 'Rondeau') is first stated and then followed by a digression called a 'Couplet'; the Ron deau is then restated and followed by a second Couplet, and th process repeated with a new Couplet for each repetition, finall ending with the Rondeau. The following, taken from one of th composer's 'Ordres', illustrates the form:

COUPERIN. 5ième Ordre. ' La Badine

RONDEAU (Principal Theme)

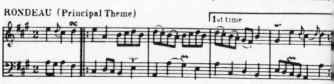

* Taken from Caldwell's *Golden Book of Modern English Verse*.

After the first Couplet a return is made to the Principal Theme, this time leading to a second Couplet beginning:

Immediately after the second Couplet there follows a restatement of the Principal Theme in the Tonic key, thus concluding the movement.

The plan is therefore:

Principal Theme *First Couplet* Principal Theme *Second Couplet* Principal Theme.

There was, in reality, no fixed number of Couplets to the early rondos which sometimes contained as many as nine appearances of the principal theme, and it therefore became necessary to limit the number of Couplets, and to have clearer definition of the form. Some of the earliest attempts in this direction are to be found in the works of Rameau (1683-1764), who may be said to have anticipated the form used by Haydn and Mozart.

Plan of a Simple Rondo*.

(a) PRINCIPAL THEME in the key of the Tonic. (The theme itself being in Binary or Ternary form.)

(b) *First Episode* in a related key.

(a²) PRINCIPAL THEME in the Tonic.

(c) *Second Episode* in another related key.

(a³) PRINCIPAL THEME in the Tonic, with or without a Coda†.

This is the plan followed in the Rondo of Haydn's Sonata in D, No. 7: the movement commences with the Subject (or Principal Theme) in the key of D.

(A) Principal Theme.

HAYDN. Rondo from Sonata in D.

This is followed by the First Episode in the key of D minor:
(B) First Episode

The Principal Theme is then restated in the Tonic:

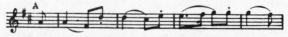

* Strictly, the essential is: that the Principal theme should occur *at least three times*.

The plan as given may be regarded as that of a Minuet with two trios thus: M.T₁. M.T₂. M., the Minuet corresponding to the Principal Theme and the Trios (T₁ and T₂) to the first and second Episodes.

† Coda (literally a 'tail-piece'), something added on for the sake of completeness.

The Second Episode (c) commences thus:

The Principal Theme is again restated, and concludes the movement.

Other examples of the Simple Rondo are to be found in the sonatas of Haydn and Mozart*. In these it will be noticed that the episodes provide greater contrast of key and of thematic material than may be seen in the early rondos of Couperin.

SONATA-FORM

Originally, a ' Sonata '† was a piece of music for an instrument, or a body of instruments, irrespective of the form of the music. Since Haydn and Mozart the term has been used for a composition for *one* or *two* solo instruments.

A modern sonata consists generally of two or more movements, of which the first is usually an Allegro designed on the particular plan, known variously as First-movement form, Sonata-Allegro form, or simply as Sonata-form‡. The following is the usual order of movements.

    (i) Allegro in *Sonata- or First-movement form.*

    (ii) A slow movement.

    (iii) Minuet and Trio, or Scherzo and Trio.

    (iv) Finale, a quick movement.

* See also the Pianoforte Rondo in A minor by Mozart (K.511). In Beethoven's Sonatas, the Modern or Sonata-Rondo is the more usual form (see p. 198).

† The term comes from the Italian ' sonare ', *to play*; it was used in contrast to ' cantare ', *to sing*. (Cf. ' cantata ', a composition for voices.)

‡ Generally referred to as *Sonata-form.*

Sonata- or First-movement form.

A movement in Sonata-form consists of three parts, viz.: (i) the Exposition, (ii) Development, (iii) Recapitulation. As an example we may take the first movement of Mozart's Pianoforte Sonata in C (K.309).

The Exposition.

This extends from the commencement of the movement up to the Double-bar, where the repeat marks indicate that the whole of the Exposition is to be played twice. The section commences with the First Subject in C major—a broad statement consisting of seven bars repeated and extended to make altogether twenty-one bars ending in the key of the Tonic.

MOZART. Sonata in C major.

After the First Subject the music leads through a *bridge* or modulatory passage, in which the key changes from C to G major, beginning thus:

Ending:

A Second Subject now appears in the new key:

This ends with a full close in the key of the Dominant (G major), reaching a double-bar at the end of the Exposition.

The *Development* begins immediately after the double-bar, and the ideas first presented in the Exposition are now treated in new and varied ways. A theme may be harmonized differently, or the composer may resort to new forms of accompaniment, or he may apply the devices of Imitation and Counterpoint to the subject-matter of the Exposition.

Mozart begins the Development section of his sonata thus:

i.e., with a presentation of the opening bars (originally major) in the Dominant minor key. The section continues for 35 bars, and is derived mainly from the material of the First Subject.

The Recapitulation.

There is no double-bar to mark the end of the Development, but the music is made to lead back to the First Subject in the Tonic key. It is the reappearance of the First Subject in the home key which indicates the commencement of the Recapitulation. The First subject now appears thus:

The 'bridge passage' (modified) now leads to the Second Subject in the Tonic key, and in this particular sonata Mozart inverts the theme so as to appear in the left hand instead of the right.

The movement ends with a short Coda based on the opening of the First Subject: this serves to emphasize the Tonic and to establish a sense of finality.

Plan of a First-movement (Sonata-form).

Exposition	Development	Recapitulation
1st Subject—*Tonic.*	Treatment of subject-matter under new conditions of rhythm, key, etc.	**1st Subject**—*Tonic.*
Bridge.		Bridge.
2nd Subject—*Dominant.*		**2nd Subject**—*Tonic.*
Codetta, or Short Coda.		Coda.

Notes on Sonata-form.

1. The two subjects in a First-movement are usually contrasted in style, the first being shorter and more strongly marked in character than the second, which is usually more melodic*.

2. The key of the Second Subject is bound by convention to that of the First. If the key of the First Subject be major, that of the Second will be the *Dominant* of the first key; if the First Subject be in a *minor* key, that of the Second subject will be the Relative major†.

3. An 'Introduction'‡ sometimes precedes the entry of the First Subject, its purpose being merely to prepare the ground for what is to come. It may, or may not, incorporate some important melodic or other features of the movement which it precedes, but in either case it must be regarded as *structurally independent*.

4. The use of a 'Coda' (literally a tail-piece) at the end of a movement, and elsewhere, has become a recognized feature of the modern sonata.

5. An abridged Sonata-form (called 'Modified Sonata-form') is sometimes used by composers, whereby the Development section is omitted. The plan is particularly suitable for 'Sonatinas' or sonatas of smaller dimensions.

* In later sonatas the Second Subject will often be found to be made up of *two*, or more, well-defined sections. Modern writers often prefer to use *first* and *second Group* (respectively) when referring to the subjects of a sonata.

† In Beethoven's Sonatas (and later) there is greater freedom in the choice of keys for the Second Subject.

‡ See Beethoven's Pianoforte Sonatas: Op. 13 in C minor; Op. 78 in F♯ major; Op. 81a in E♭ major; and Op. 111 in C minor.

The older Rondo, with its squareness and somewhat obvious plan, does not seem to have commended itself wholeheartedly to Beethoven, who frequently preferred a more organic and highly developed form, called *Sonata-Rondo**. The following will enable the two forms to be compared:

Simple Rondo	*Sonata-Rondo*
a. Principal Subject—*Tonic*.	**a.** Principal Subject—*Tonic*.
b. First Episode—*Dominant*.†	**b.** Second Subject—*Dominant*.
a². Principal Subject—*Tonic*.	**a²**. Principal Subject—*Tonic*.
c. Second Episode—*Another related key*.	**c.** Episode, often with some kind of thematic development, passing through various keys.
a³. Principal Subject—*Tonic*. Coda (optional).	**a³**. Principal Subject—*Tonic*.
	b². Second Subject in *Tonic*.
	a⁴. Principal Subject in Tonic, usually with *Coda*.

As an example of the form we may take the last movement of the Sonata in C, Op. 2, No. 3 (Beethoven).

The movement opens with the Principal Subject in the Tonic, thus:

BEETHOVEN.

It will be noticed that the character of the above is quite different from that of the First Subject in a Sonata, being structurally simpler and much more straightforward.

* The form was, of course, *foreshadowed* by Haydn and Mozart.
† Usually, though not invariably.

The Second Subject (**b**) is in the key of the Dominant:

A return to the Principal Subject now follows, leading to an Episode based upon this theme*.

Some development of the above now takes place and leads to a return of the Principal Subject in the Tonic, followed by the Second Subject, also in the Tonic:

The Final section follows, consisting of the Principal Subject restated several times, and ending with it in the following inverted form:

* In some cases the Episode may develop material already heard.

In some respects the form of the Modern Rondo keeps closely to that of the First-movement or Sonata-form:

Sonata First-movement	Sonata-Rondo
Exposition.	
a. First Subject—*Tonic.*	**a.** Principal Subject—*Tonic.*
b. Second Subject—*Dominant.*	**b.** Second Subject—*Dominant.*
With or without *Codetta* based on First Subject.	**a².** Principal Subject—*restated in full*.
Development.	*Episode.*
Usually opens with a 'motive' or 'figure' from the First Subject. A section of free modulation.	Tonality (or key system) more settled than in the Development of a Sonata-form.
Recapitulation.	
a². First Subject—*Tonic.*	**a³.** Principal Subject—*Tonic.*
b². Second Subject—*Tonic.*	**b².** Second Subject—*Tonic.*
Frequently with a Coda alluding to First Subject.	**a⁴.** Principal Subject, usually with a *Coda* based upon it.

DIFFERENCES BETWEEN FIRST-MOVEMENT FORM AND SONATA-RONDO

1. In the Rondo the second appearance of the Principal Subject (before the Episode) is almost always *complete*: what corresponds to this in a Sonata First-movement is the Codetta (where found) which merely *refers* to the First Subject.

2. The Episode of the Rondo is more settled as to shape and key-system than the Development Section in a Sonata-form.

3. In the Rondo the Principal Subject is rhythmically the simpler because it has to bear frequent repetition. In Sonata-form the First Subject is the more distinctive in its ideas and content, and is usually shorter in length than the Second Subject.

4. In the Rondo the Tonic key is more evenly distributed throughout the movement than in Sonata form, due to the repetition of the Principal Subject in the Tonic.

THE REMAINING MOVEMENTS IN A SONATA

Other movements of the Sonata remain to be mentioned, viz. the Slow movement, Variations, the Minuet and Trio, and the Scherzo and Trio.

The Slow Movement represents the ' elegiac ' element of a Sonata, it lays special stress on the qualities of style and sentiment. Its structure is sometimes that of a Ternary form*, and sometimes a Rondo†. In consequence of its tempo it will be shorter in (written) length, in order to provide a balance of duration with the other movements. It will also tend to elaboration and variation of phrase, because there is a danger of slow melodic phrases becoming too uniform and stagnant.

The *Air with Variations* sometimes takes the place of the Slow Movement, in which case it is not usual to have more than six variations of the theme. (See: *Beethoven*, Pianoforte Sonata in G, Op. 14, No. 2.)

The Minuet and Trio—The Scherzo.

The Minuet and Trio are two movements which usually occur together in the sonatas of Haydn and Mozart. They are genial movements, full of grace and charm, and played in the order described on page 188. In Beethoven's sonatas their place is frequently taken by the Scherzo and Trio—two movements of similar structure to the Minuet and Trio but markedly different in character, and usually full of humour and good-natured fun‡. It is in this sense that the Scherzo must be regarded as one of the important innovations introduced by Beethoven, although sometimes (e.g. in the Fifth Symphony) it assumes a more serious character.

VARIATION-FORM

In Variation-form a theme is first announced and then repeated with modifications of melody and harmony, etc.

The earliest instances of the form consisted of a chain of themes each with a single variation. This gave place later to the ' set ' of variations (often called ' *Doubles* ') and to the type of variations known as the ' *Ground-bass* ' or ' Basso ostinato ', in which the theme was used as a bass, being repeated over and over again with a changing superstructure of harmony and of melody. The following is the opening of a movement by Purcell illustrating the procedure adopted.

* Often called Aria or Song-form in a slow movement.

† Hadow, *Sonata Form.*

‡ Scherzo—Italian for *jest.* The term was, of course, used by Haydn in some of his Quartets, and by other composers.

This method of treating a theme in the bass came to be used for certain dance-movements—the Chaconne and the Passacaglia. Handel used these forms freely in his Suites for Harpsichord; and Bach's great 'Passacaglia in C minor' for organ is built upon the following 'ground', repeated twenty times: J. S. BACH

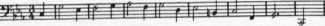

Beethoven shows a superb mastery of the art of variation-writing, and his set of Variations to 'The Men of Prometheus' illustrates the chief devices used by composers.

The theme is announced in the key of E♭ major, and is in Binary form. BEETHOVEN.

In the course of the Variations the following devices occur:

1. The outline of the melody varied, harmonic basis retained:

2. Melody reharmonized:

3. The outline of the melody completely broken up:

4. The character of the theme changed by varying the rhythm and tempo:

5. A complete departure from the theme except in respect of harmony or cadences:

6. The theme presented in Canon*:

7. The bass of the theme used as the Subject of a fugue:

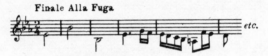

Finale Alla Fuga

etc.

Beethoven frequently makes his last variation serve as a kind of Coda to the whole movement, thus overcoming any feeling of squareness which tends to arise out of the continued repetition of the theme.

THE FUGUE†

This is a composition for instruments or for voices, based usually on a *single* theme (generally short and definite in character) called the *Fugue Subject*.

BACH. Fugue in C major.

Subject

For convenience in explanation we may divide a Fugue into three parts, viz.: (i) the Exposition, (ii) the Middle Section, and (iii) the Final Section.

* See p. 209.
† Note also: (a) *Fughetta*—a diminutive type of fugue, with much shortened middle-section.
(b) *Fugato*—a passage in the *style* of a fugal exposition, but without observing the strict rules of Subject and Answer.

The *Exposition* commences with the Subject given out in one voice ' or part, and answered by another. The Answer consists of the notes of the Subject reproduced in the Dominant, i.e., a Perfect 5th higher or a Perfect 4th lower: when every note of the Answer conforms to this principle, it is said to be *real*.

When the Subject commences with the Dominant, it must be answered by the Tonic; and a leap from Dominant to Tonic will be answered by a leap from Tonic to Dominant; the Answer in such a case is said to be *tonal*.

The Subject having been answered, a third voice enters with it again, and this, in turn, is answered by a fourth, etc., according to the number of voices. When each voice has entered with the Subject or Answer, the Exposition is ordinarily said to be complete*.

The following is the Exposition of Bach's Fugue in C minor. Notice how each voice, when it has completed the Subject, continues with the *Counter-subject* above or below the Subject in another part.

* It is sometimes followed by a *Counter-exposition* in which the voices enter in a different order, the Subject being taken up by the voice which previously had the Answer, and *vice versa*. The order of keys is the same as in the (first) Exposition.

Bach. Fugue in C minor (Book I, No. 2)

An extra, or *redundant* entry, will sometimes be made by the *first* voice (after all the voices have entered) enabling the last voice to proceed with the Counter-subject and show it inverted if desired.   See Bach's ' 48 ' (Book I, No. 23).

The Middle Section.

The Exposition being complete, a modulatory passage (' Episode ') leads the music away from the Tonic to the Middle Section of the fugue, where Subject or Answer, or both, may re-enter in a new key.   The following is an ' Episode ' leading from C minor to the relative major, in which the composer makes use of figures and material derived from the Subject or Counter-subject.

Bach. Fugue in C minor.

Subject in E♭ major

When one voice has re-entered, it may be followed by others with the Subject or Answer. The fugue then passes through another 'Episode' into a new key (in which further entries are made), and the process repeated at length. A return is then made to the Tonic, or home-key, for the Final Section.

Final Section.

It is here that a fugue usually reaches its climax, through various cumulative devices such as *Stretto*, *Pedal*, etc.*

BACH. Fugue in D major.

Subject

Answer

Close Stretto.
BACH. Fugue in D major.

Answer

Use of a Pedal in the Bass.
BACH. Fugue in C minor.

Fine

* *Stretto* –The closing together of the entries of Subject or Answer.

Other devices found in the course of a fugue:

(i) *Augmentation.*

BACH. ' Forty-eight ' (Book II, No. 2).

(Answer by inverse movement)

(ii) *Diminution.*

(iii) *Inversion of Subject.*

BACH. Fugue in D minor ˙

The Fugue form has been freely used by composers in the choruses of large vocal works such as the Oratorio and the Mass. Such choruses will sometimes be found to be Double or Triple fugues, i.e., fugues with two or three subjects, as in the ' Kyrie ' of Mozart's ' Requiem ', or the chorus ' Glory to his name for ever ' from Haydn's ' Creation '*.

* Instances of Double fugues for *instruments* may also be noticed: e.g. Bach's Organ Fugue in C minor and D. Scarlatti's Harpsichord Fugue in D minor.

THE CANON

In a simple Canon, a voice leads with a given melody. Whilst it is proceeding, another voice enters with the melody at the same or a different pitch.

TALLIS'S CANON.

The 'Direct' signs (𝕨) indicate the Bass to be sung with the Canon.

In this particular case the second voice commences an octave below the first voice, and a bar later. The first voice continues the melody to the end, the second voice imitating it strictly at the same interval until it, in turn, completes the melody. The above is described as a Canon 2 in 1 at the octave.

In the next example, *three* voices take part (3 in 1).

WILLIAM BYRD.

The following is the opening of a Canon with two subjects (4 in 2).

BACH. Organ Prelude on ' In dulci jubilo '.

Finite and Infinite Canon.

Canons are of two kinds—a *Finite* canon being one in which the ' Antecedent' or leading voice drops out on completing the melody or continues with a free part until the 'Consequent'

209

ends. An *Infinite* canon returns to the beginning without a break enabling it to be continued at will for any length of time

Canon by Inversion.

Sometimes the ' Consequent ' imitates the leading voice in strict inversion; this makes a *Canon by Inversion*.

KLENGEL. ' Forty-eight Canons and Fugues.

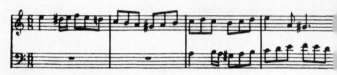

The ' Round ' and the ' Catch '.

The *Round* may be described as a *Canon-in-the-Unison* composed usually for three or for four voices*. The music is rarely ever written out in full, but in score—'placing the phrases one above the other, and indicating at the beginning and end of the lines the order in which they are to be sung† '.

PURCELL.

The figure at the end of each line indicates the line to be sung next.

* There are also interesting specimens of Rounds for five and six voices by Mozart and Beethoven, etc. (See *Clarendon Song Book*, VI.)

† Quoted from Prout.

The *Catch* was at one time a popular form of Round in which the main interest was in the play of words which, by the placing of the syllables, were made to suggest other words to the listener's ears.

DANCE MOVEMENTS: THE SUITE

In the Elizabethan Collections for Virginal we find dances such as the Pavan, Galliard, Almain, Branle, etc., grouped in ' sets ' with the obvious intention of matching together a number of movements contrasted in style and character. These pieces were followed about a hundred years later by the ' Ordres ' of Couperin, in which the composer sometimes has a particular sequence of dance-movements, viz.: Allemande, Courante, Saraband and Gigue.

This practice of grouping together a number of dance-movements found favour with composers, and came to be used by Handel and Bach in their Suites, and in the Partitas of the latter composer.

In the Suites and Partitas it became the custom to have three principal movements, viz.: the *Allemande*, the *Courante*, and the *Saraband*, and to end the Suite generally with a *Gigue*. After the three principal movements (i.e., before the Gigue), the composer was at liberty to include one or more short movements called *Intermezzi*, or Galanterien, and in this category were included the Minuet, Gavotte, Bourrée, Passepied, Loure, Passacaglia, Rondeau, Air, etc. It was usual for the first of the Intermezzi movements to be in a Triple time and for the remainder to be in Common time. Any one of the Intermezzo movements could be followed by another of the same character, and in that case the added movement was called an *Alternativo*. Thus we frequently have in a Suite a Minuet I and a Minuet II, the second Minuet being an ' Alternativo '.

The plan of a Suite was therefore:

Allemande ⎫
Courante ⎬ Principal Movements.
Saraband ⎭

Minuet, $\frac{3}{4}$ time ⎫
Bourrée, etc. ⎬ Intermezzi (Optional Movements).
Air, etc. ⎭

Gigue—usually the concluding movement.

Sometimes a Suite would commence with a *Prelude*, being in some cases 'a mere flourish', as with Handel and the earlier Suite-writers, and in others (e.g., Bach's *English Suites**) a quite massive and imposing composition.

The characteristic features of the various movements are as follows:

The Allemande.

In its earliest form the Allemande began with the first beat of the bar, but later this was always preceded by one or three semiquavers.

BACH. Allemande from First French Suite.

The Courante and Corrente.

The second *essential* movement of the Suite is to be found in two forms, viz.: the Courante (French) and the Corrente (Italian). In a true Courante the rhythm at the cadences (and sometimes throughout a movement) is made to alternate between $\frac{6}{4}$ and $\frac{3}{2}$ time.

BACH. Courante (II) from ' English Suite ', No. 1 in A.

A feature of the Corrente† is the flowing rhythm maintained consistently throughout the movement. It is rhythmically a simpler form than the Courante, and written in $\frac{3}{4}$ time.

* Each of Bach's *English Suites* has a prelude: the *French Suites* have none.

† Often wrongly called a *Courante* by Bach.

BACH. Corrente* from Fifth French Suite.

The Saraband.

A slow, stately dance in $\frac{3}{2}$ or $\frac{3}{4}$ time, often with marked emphasis on the second beat of each bar. The movement commences on the first beat of the bar.

HANDEL. 'Lascia ch'io pianga'

The Passacaglia.

A form of variation on a Ground-bass: an early example by Purcell is given on page 201.

The Gavotte and the Musette.

The Gavotte was a lively dance in Duple time, with a somewhat square rhythm, and commencing on the third crotchet of the bar. It was an Intermezzo movement, and was frequently followed by a Musette† (or second Gavotte) with a Pedal-bass.

Gavotte.   BACH. English Suite, No. III.

Musette (or Gavotte II).   BACH. English Suite, No. III.

---

* Actually, it is called a Courante.

† So named after the Musette or bagpipe, with its drone or persistent accompanying note.

The Bourrée.

A smooth, easy-flowing movement in ₵ time commencing (unlike the Gavotte) on the last crotchet of the bar.

BACH. Fifth French Suite.

The Gigue.

A lively movement, probably of English origin*, found with various time-signatures: $\frac{3}{8}$, $\frac{3}{4}$, $\frac{6}{8}$, $\frac{9}{8}$, $\frac{12}{8}$, etc. Its distinguishing, though not invariable characteristic, is a continuous triplet subdivision of the beats, not infrequently with fugal treatment of the main idea. It gives the Suite a spritely and vivacious ending.

HANDEL. From the 'Sixth Suite' of Second Collection.

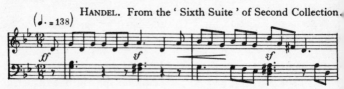

The Prelude.

An introductory movement without any prescribed form.

PURCELL. Prelude to Suite

The Partitas.

These were a collection of Suites by J. S. Bach which appeared between 1726 and 1731. A feature of the six Partitas is that each begins with a different kind of movement, viz.: No. 1, Prelude; No. 2, Sinfonia; No. 3, Fantasia; No. 4, Overture; No. 5, Préambule; No. 6, Toccata.

* Cf. the English 'Jig', to which it is probably related.

The style of the Partitas might be said to be slighter than that of the majority of the other works of Bach, and it has been suggested that they were written so as to be popular in the best sense. In Fuller Maitland's words*: ' If it were desired to introduce a partially educated musician to the world of Bach's music, no better gateway could be found than the first Partita as a whole '

THE OVERTURE, SYMPHONY AND CONCERTO

These three terms were at one time used for any composition for a body of instruments, without any particular reference to the form of the music. An early instance of the term ' Symphony ' is to be found in Peri's opera ' Euridice ', where it is used for the music played by way of an introduction to the drama. With the development of opera, the term ' Overture ' came to be applied in a similar connection, but also for instrumental pieces as well, until by about 1700 two distinct forms of Overture had emerged, viz.: the French form, said to have originated with Lully, and the Italian, due mainly to the influence of Alessandro Scarlatti. The two forms may be compared thus:

French Overture	*Italian Overture* (Sinfonia)
(1) Introduction—slow and dignified.	(1) Allegro—a quick movement frequently fugal in style.
(2) Allegro—usually fugal in style.	(2) Slow movement.
(3) A stately movement such as a Minuet.	(3) Finale—a quick movement.

The overture to Handel's ' Samson ' is an instance of the French form, the movements, in order, being as follows: Andante–Allegro–Menuetto. Bach's Clavier Concerto in D minor follows the Italian plan: Allegro–Adagio–Allegro†.

In course of time it came to be realized that an Overture could be played as an independent composition, i.e., complete in itself, and musicians began to adopt an Overture-plan for their instrumental compositions‡. It was the Italian form which appealed

* J. A. Fuller Maitland, *Keyboard Suites*.

† Most of Bach's Concertos are on the Italian plan.

‡ Evidence of this is to be found in the ' Symphonies ' of J. C. Bach, Stamitz, and others, who used the Overture-plan.

more generally to composers, and it was this which paved the way for the symphonies of Haydn and Mozart. By about the middle of the eighteenth century the term ' Symphony ' was used in the strict sense of a cycle of movements for an orchestra, of which the first was in regular Sonata-form. After Haydn and Mozart expansion of symphonic design came through Beethoven and Brahms, but with few modern exceptions the plan and structure of the Symphony have remained the same to the present day.

The Modern Overture is a composition for orchestra consisting of *one* movement only, and written in Sonata first-movement form. The Exposition is never repeated as in true Sonata-form and the movement is sometimes preceded by a Slow Introduction Beethoven's ' Egmont ' is a good example: it commences with an Introduction leading to an Allegro in First-movement form, and ends with an extended Coda.

The form has been frequently used for the instrumental introduction to an oratorio or an opera, as in Mendelssohn' ' St Paul ' and Mozart's ' Figaro ', as well as for independent compositions intended purely as concert pieces (Concert-overtures), e.g., Mendelssohn's 'Hebrides Overture' and the ' Overture to a Midsummer Night's Dream '*.

The Concerto is a composition for a solo instrument with orchestral accompaniment, and consists usually of three movements†.

The First-movement has a *Double Exposition* and commences with a *tutti* passage (for orchestra alone), in which both subjects are first announced in the key of the movement. The solo instrument then enters with the Principal theme and gives out the subjects in their respective keys. Both the Development and the Recapitulation commence similarly with *tutti* passages which prepare the way for each subsequent re-entry of the solo instrument.

At the close of the Recapitulation a pause in the solo part (following a $^6_4$ chord on the Dominant) indicates that the soloist

* Sometimes described as ' Programme music ' on account of the story or situation which the pieces illustrate or suggest.

† Concertos are also written for more than one solo instrument, being then described as Double, Triple concertos, etc., as the case may be. In such cases the construction of the work is similar to that for a single instrument.

is to continue with a *Cadenza*, or solo passage, either extemporized or previously prepared by himself. The purpose of the Cadenza is to enable the performer to display his skill as an executant and improvisator, and to give the movement the necessary flourish towards the close. Termination of the Cadenza is indicated by a prolonged trill on the Dominant thus:

Beethoven
Concerto in C min.

This prepares for the re-entry of the orchestra, which then proceeds to the end of the movement with, or without, the solo instrument.

The second and third movements resemble those of a Sonata—the one being a slow movement and the other usually a Rondo. The Cadenza, although not regarded as essential, is frequently introduced in the last movement, but in considerably shortened form.

In essentials, the modern Concerto form may be said to have been settled by Mozart, but certain innovations were introduced by Beethoven, e.g., the shortening of the opening *tutti* passage, the writing out of the Cadenza in full, and the linking up of the last two movements into one. With later composers the tendency has been to give greater prominence to the orchestra, and, in some cases, to do away altogether with the Cadenza. (See Mendelssohn's and Brahms's Pianoforte Concertos.)

Historically, the term Concerto is of considerable interest, having first been used for a series of motets* for voices and organ, and later for compositions for a group of instruments alone. It is in this latter sense that it was used by Handel and Bach, who sometimes treated all the instruments equally, and sometimes in solo and accompanying groups. Some of the former's concertos have parts for two violins and violoncello, called a *Concertino*, and this group of instruments is used in contrast with the full body of strings, called *Concerto Grosso*. Bach's concertos were

* *Motet:* a kind of anthem, usually with Latin words.

frequently written for *Concertante* (solo group) and *Ripieno*—an accompanying group often consisting of strings alone.

Mention must be made of the *ad libitum* passages in some of Handel's concertos; he was the first to introduce opportunities for extemporary performance on the part of the soloist, and therefore to anticipate the modern Cadenza. Also of Bach's six Brandenburg Concertos in which *various* groups of instruments are used as 'Concertante'; they were presented by the composer to the Markgraf of Brandenburg in 1721, and have since been known by that name.

N.B.—The numbering commences with the first *complete* bar.

SONATA IN F MINOR, Op. 2, No. 1

FIRST MOVEMENT: 'Allegro'. SONATA FORM.

Exposition	Development	Recapitulation
1-8—*Principal Subject*, or First Group in F minor.	48/9-54—Material of First Group.	101-108—*First Group* in Tonic.
9-20—*Bridge*, or Transition.	55/73—Passing through B♭ minor, C minor, and reaching Dominant of A♭ major.	108/9-119—*B r i d g e, o r Transition* modified so as to end on home Dominant chord.
21-41—*Second Group* in A♭ major ending with **Λ**.	73/81—Continuation by sequence without reference to thematic material.	119-145—*Second Group*, including part of Cadence-theme (bars. 41-46), in the Tonic.
41-48—Cadence theme, or Codetta.	81-100—Dominant preparation for return of First Group, with broken pedal (bars 81-92) leading through stepwise descending bass to Recapitulation.	146-end—Coda.

REPEAT.

First Group—Contains two melodic germs, (*a*) and (*b*): both are used in the Bridge passage and in the Development.

Second Group—The opening bars are constructed out of notes of the Dominant chord—with the Minor 9th from the root.

Coda—Commences at the interruption of the expected Full close (bar 145/6): it consists of repetition of the cadential progression a step lower, leading through a crotchet passage (with cross accent) to the final cadence.

SECOND MOVEMENT: 'Adagio'. F major. ABRIDGED SONATA FORM, i.e., Sonata Form without Development.

Exposition	Recapitulation
1-16—*Principal Subject*, or First Group ending with Full close in C major.	32-47—*First Group* in Tonic. Connecting link (bar 47) leads **to:**
17-22—*Bridge*, or Transition.	48-55—*Second Group* in Tonic.
23-31—*Second Group* in C major.	56-61—Coda.

First Group—Two strains, (*a*) ending with a Full close in the Tonic and (*b*) closing into the opening bars of (*a*) modified (bar 13).

Bridge—New thematic material. In the Recapitulation it consists merely of the connecting link of seven notes (bar 47).

Coda—Consisting of cadential repetition with an echo device in last bar.

THIRD MOVEMENT: 'Menuetto' and 'Trio'. F minor and Tonic m.
MINUET AND TRIO FORM.

Menuetto

1/1-14—*First Strain* begins in F minor and ends with a Full close in A♭ major.
REPEAT.

14/15-28—*Second Strain* commences in A♭ major leading through a thrice-repeated Full close in B♭ minor (19-24) to the home Dominant.
28/9-40 — *First Strain* repeated: theme reappears in Left hand, leading to a Full close in the Tonic.
REPEAT.

Trio

40/1-50—*First Strain* in F m. modulating to C major.
REPEAT.

50/1-65—*Second Strain* mainly o. Dominant commencing with same figure as the First Strai

66-73—*First Strain* repeated (modification) ending in the T (F major).
REPEAT. Minuet Da Capo.

The movement as a whole makes a complete Ternary Form: Min. Trio-Minuet. Note the use of *Inversion* in the Trio; compare bars 41 45, 51 and 55 *et seq.* Also the shortening of the First Strain in the Recap. lation—eight bars instead of ten.

FOURTH MOVEMENT: 'Prestissimo'. F minor. SONATA FORM WITH EPISO. Development.

Exposition

1-21—*First Group* in F minor ending with Dominant preparation for C minor.
22-49—*Second Group* in C minor, closing into:
50-56—*Cadence - group*, or Codetta, based on opening bars of First Group.

Development

57-58—Final chords of Exposition re-echoed.

59-108—Episode in A♭, consisting of a new 10-bar melody repeated and followed by another new strain of 4 bars repeated, etc.

109-137—Resumption of Development.

Recapitulation

138-160—*First Grou.* Tonic.

161-192—*Second C* in Tonic.

193-196—Cadence-g. being a transpositi. Codetta to F min.

The part of a bar at the very beginning does not really belong to the Group and must be regarded as a kind of Introduction. The First G. is made up of (a) consisting of four one-bar units and (b) a fou. melody in A♭ leading on repetition to the Dominant of C minor.
The Second Group also has two sections extending respectively over 22-33/34 and 34/35-49/50.
Note the inversion of the left- and right-hand parts in bars 193 *et se.* compared with bars 50 *et seq.*—the triplet quavers in the Cadence-g. now appear in the right hand and the chords in the left hand.

SONATA IN B FLAT MAJOR, Op. 22, No. 1

FIRST MOVEMENT: ' Allegro con brio '. SONATA FORM.

Exposition	*Development*	*Recapitulation*
1-11—*First Group*, ending with Dominant close.	68/9-127—Material of opening bars and Codetta—mainly the latter.	127/8-138—*First Group* in Tonic.
12-21 — *Bridge*, or Transition.		138/9-152—*Bridge*.
22-61—*Second Group* in F major closing into a self-repeating theme over a tonic pedal (56-61).		153-199—*Second Group* in Tonic, being bars 22-68 restated and ending with Codetta similarly transposed.
62-68 — Cadence-phrase or Codetta ending with a Full close in the Dominant.		
REPEAT.		

First Group—Consisting of two sections: (*a*) an ' abrupt figure in disguised thirds '* and (*b*) a four-bar cantabile.
Bridge—Commencing with (*a*).
Second Group—In three sections (i) bars 22-30; (ii) 30-56; (iii) 56-61 (with Tonic pedal).
Codetta—A rhythmic scale passage in double-octaves followed by a passing reference to (*a*) of the First Group.

SECOND MOVEMENT: ' Adagio con molta espressione '. E flat. SONATA FORM.

Exposition	*Development*	*Recapitulation*
1-12—*First Group* in E♭ (eight bars with cadential repetition).	31-46—Use of opening figure of First Group and the following from the end of bar 4.	47-57—*First Group* in Tonic.
12/13-17 — *Bridge*, or Transition.		57/58-64—*Bridge*.
18-27—*Second Group* in Dominant (B♭).		65-77—*Second Group* in Tonic.
27-30.—Cadence-phrase or Codetta.		

The Bridge passage is not constructed out of previous material, but consists of a new two-bar theme closing in the Tonic and answered by a further three bars leading to the Dominant.
The Second Group commences over a Tonic pedal with imitative lower parts.
In the Recapitulation the last two bars of the First Group are omitted; compare with bars 1-12.

---

*Tovey, *A Companion to Beethoven's Sonatas.*

THIRD MOVEMENT: ' Menuetto' and ' Minore '. MINUET AND TRIO FORM.

Menuetto, B♭	Minore, G minor
$\frac{3}{4}$/1-8—*First Strain* commencing in B♭ and ending with Full close in Tonic. *REPEAT*.	30/31-38—Eight-bar strain ending with Full close in the Dominant.
8/9-16—*Second Strain*, closing on the home Dominant.	38/39-46—The same strain taken up by the upper parts in turn, first in the Subdominant and then in the Tonic, with resumption of the First Strain in the bass (bar 42/43) leading in four bars to a Full close in the Tonic.
16/17-24—*First Strain* restated with a more florid bass, leading to the home Tonic.	
24/25-30—Codetta. *REPEAT*.	*REPEAT*. Minuet Da Capo.

Taken as a whole, the movement is a complete Ternary Form, thus: Menuetto-Minore-Menuetto.

FOURTH MOVEMENT: ' Rondo '. Allegretto. B flat major. SONATA-RONDO FORM.

First Part	Second Part	Third Part
$\frac{2}{4}$/1-18—*Principal Subject* in B♭ ending with Full close in Tonic.	67/68-111 — *Second Episode* in complete three-part form, with Development.	111/112-129—*Principal Subject* in Tonic.
		129/130-164 — *Return to Second Subject* (modified) in the Tonic.
18/19-49—*Transition* merging into *Second Subject* in F major.		164/5-182 — *Final return of Principal Subject* in Tonic.
49/50-67—*Principal Subject* in B♭ (First return).		182/3-199—*Coda*.

Principal Subject—An eight-bar strain closing in the Dominant and repeated in octaves, with modification so as to end in the Tonic.

Second Subject—Commences at bar 22/23.

Episode—In complete recapitulatory form:
    72-80—New theme in F minor.
    80/1-94—Figure of bars 18/19-20 developed.
    95-103—Recapitulation of bars 72-80 in B♭ minor.

Final return—Restatement of Principal Subject in decorated form, with triplet subdivision of beats.

Coda—Making use of the rhythmic material of bar 18/19, and concluding with the notes of the Principal Subject worked in close imitation.

CHRONOLOGY OF COMPOSERS—WITH CHIEF WORKS

PERIOD OF UNACCOMPANIED CHORAL MUSIC

PALESTRINA (1525-94). Italian. Born at Palestrina, near Rome.
Compositions include a large number of Masses for 4, 5, 6,
and 8 voices ; Motets for 4 to 8 voices and six for 12 voices ;
Offertories, Lamentations, Magnificats, and Psalm-settings
for 12 voices.

    Missa Brevis
    Missa Papae Marcelli
    Cantiones Sacrae
    Spiritual Madrigals (61)
    Secular Madrigals (95)

BYRD, William (1543-1623). English.

Vocal Music.

' Psalmes, Sonets and Songs of Sadnes and Pietie ' (3-6 parts).
Masses and Madrigals.
Canon: ' Non nobis Domine '.

Instrumental Music.

Sets of pieces for Virginals (to be found in ' Lady Neville's
Book ', the ' Fitzwilliam Virginal Book ', and in the
' Parthenia ').

THE BEGINNING OF OPERA AND ORATORIO

MONTEVERDI (1567-1643). Italian.

Operas and Ballets (18).

' La favola d'Orfeo '.
' Arianna '.
' Il ritorno d'Ulisse in patria ' (incorporating *bel canto da capo
aria* and *recitativo secco*).

Religious Music.

Motets, Madrigali spirituali, Masses (about 130).

Madrigals for 1, 2, 3, 4, 5 *and* 6 *voices.* (Over 200, in 12 Compila-
tions including the *Canzonette, Scherzi musicali*, etc.).

Spiritual Parodies and other smaller works.

' Lamento d'Arianna '.

PURCELL, Henry (1658 (or 59)-1695).   English.
Operas (6).
   ' Dido and Aeneas ' ; ' Dioclesian ' ; ' King Arthur ' ; ' The
      Faery Queen ' ; ' The Indian Queen ' ; ' The Tempest '.
Incidental Music and Songs for Plays (44).
Anthems (13), *Verse Anthems* (49) *and Services* (3).
   ' Save me, O God ' (Anthem).
   ' O Praise God in His Holiness ' (Verse Anthem).
   ' Te Deum and Jubilate in D '.
Choral Music.
   Festival Odes (25)—' Ode on St. Cecilia's Day '.
   Welcome-Songs for solo voice, chorus and orchestra (9).
   Cantatas for solo voices and instruments (9).
   Three-part Songs, Vocal Duets, and Songs with Continuo (48).
Music for Strings with, or without Continuo.
   Fantasias ; Overtures : Sonatas of 3, 4 and 5 parts.
Harpsichord Music.
   Suites (8) ; Miscellaneous Pieces (49) including Collections,
     e.g. ' Musick's Handmaid '.
Organ Music.
        PERIOD OF COUNTERPOINT AND HARMONY
BACH, John Sebastian (1685-1750). German. Born at Eisenach.
Church Music.
   Passion according to St Matthew.
   Passion according to St John.
   Mass in B minor.
   Magnificat in D.
   The Christmas Oratorio.
   Over 230 Church Cantatas.
Clavier Works and Chamber Music.
   Two- and three-part Inventions.
   French Suites.
   English Suites.
   Partitas.
   The ' 48 Preludes and Fugues '. (Das Wohltemperirte Clavier.)
   The Art of Fugue.
   Sonatas for Clavier and Violin.
   Sonatas for Clavier and Flute.
   Concertos for various instruments.
   Six ' Brandenburg ' Concertos.

Organ Works
  Toccatas, Preludes and Fugues.
  Sonatas.
  Preludes on Chorales.
HANDEL, George Frideric, b. Halle 1685, d. London 1759.
Operas.
  Italian (39), e.g. ' Roderigo ' ; ' Berenice '.
  German (3), ' Almira '.
Oratorios and Masques (13).
  ' Acis and Galatea ' (Masque) ; ' Semele ' (English Opera-
    Oratorio) ; ' Saul ' ; ' Israel in Egypt ' ; ' Messiah ' ;
    ' Samson ' ; ' Judas Maccabeus ' ; ' Joshua ' ; ' Solomon ' ;
    ' Jeptha '.
Other Choral Works with Orchestra.
  ' Alexander's Feast ' ; Settings of the ' Te Deum ' (*Utrecht,
    Dettingen*, etc.) ; Chandos Anthems (11).
Orchestral Works.
  ' Water Music ', ' Music for the Royal Fireworks ' ; Concertos
    and Concerti Grossi ; Overtures.
Chamber Music.
  Sonatas (with keyboard instrument) for Violin, for Flute, etc.
  Trio-sonatas for various groups of instruments.
Harpsichord Music.
  Suites, Fugues, Sonatas, etc.
Organ Concertos (21).
GLUCK, C. Willibald von (1714-87).   German.
Operas.
  Italian (34) : ' Orfeo ', ' Alceste '.
  French (19) : ' Alceste '*.
                 ' Iphigenie en Aulide '.
                 ' Armide '.
                 ' Iphigenie en Tauride '.
      (* Italian *and* French.)

HAYDN, Joseph (1732-1809). Austrian. Born at Rohrau.
Symphonies.
> One hundred and four (authenticated), including the twelve 'Salomon' Symphonies, e.g., the 'Surprise' in G and the 'Clock' in D.

Pianoforte Sonatas (53).
Chamber Music.
> Trios, Quartets, etc.

Oratorios.
> 'The Creation.'
> 'The Seasons.'
> 'The Seven Words from the Cross' (arr. from String Quartet).

Operas. Unimportant.

MOZART, Wolfgang Amadeus (1756-1791). Austrian. Born in Salzburg.
Symphonies (41).
> 'Paris' in D (K.297), No. 31.
> 'Haffner' in D (K.385), No. 35.
> 'Prague' in D (K.504), No. 38.
> E flat (K.543), No. 39.
> G minor (K.550), No. 40.
> 'Jupiter' in C (K.551), No. 41.
> (K.—signifies the order of appearance of the composition in Köchel's chronological catalogue of Mozart's works : *No.* — indicates the numbering of each symphony in the Breitkopf und Härtel Edition).

Operas.
> 'Idomeneo' (Opera seria).
> 'Die Entführung . . .' (Musical play).
> 'The Marriage of Figaro' (Musical Comedy).
> 'Don Giovanni' (Light drama).
> 'Così fan Tutte' (Opera buffa).
> 'The Magic Flute' (German Opera).

Solo Instruments with Orchestra.
> Concertos, etc. for Violin (18), Pianoforte (30), Horn (4).
> 'Symphonia Concertante' for Violin, Viola and Orchestra.

Church Music.
> 'Requiem.' Masses and motets.
> Pianoforte Sonatas (17).

Chamber Music.
> Sonatas for Violin and Pianoforte (about 35).
> Piano Trios (8) ; String Quartets (23) ; Piano Quartets (2).
> Serenade : 'Eine kleine Nachtmusik' ; Divertimenti.

BEETHOVEN, Ludwig van (1770-1827). German. Born at Bonn.

Symphonies (9).
    No. 1 in C, No. 2 in D, No. 3 in E♭ (' Eroica '), No. 4 in B♭, No. 5 in C minor, No. 6 in F (' Pastoral '), No. 7 in A, No. 8 in F, No. 9 in D minor (' Choral ').

Overtures (9).
    Including the ' Coriolan ', ' Egmont ', ' Leonora ' (Nos. 1, 2, and 3), ' The Ruins of Athens.'

Concertos (5).
    Pianoforte—The ' Emperor ' Concerto.
    Violin Concerto, etc.

Chamber Music.
    Septet for Strings and Wind.
    Trios, Quartets, etc.
    Sonatas for Violin and Pianoforte.

Pianoforte Music.
    Thirty-two Sonatas.
    Twenty-one Sets of Variations.

Vocal Music.
    Mass in C.
    Mass in D (' Missa Solemnis ').

Opera.
    ' Fidelio.'

Periods of Composition

First Period—Leading up to about Op. 50, showing the influence of Haydn and Mozart, including :
    Pianoforte Sonatas (the ' Pathétique ' and the ' Moonlight ').
    Symphonies Nos. 1 and 2.
    ' Kreutzer ' Sonata for Violin and Pianoforte.
    Septet for Strings and Wind.

Second Period (Op. 50-90 approx.).
    ' The Waldstein ' (Op. 53) and ' Appassionata ' (Op. 57) Pianoforte Sonatas.
    Symphonies Nos. 3 (' Eroica '), 4, 5, 6, 7 and 8.
    ' Coriolan ' and ' Egmont ' overtures.
    The opera ' Fidelio.'
    The ' Rasoumoffsky ' Quartets.
    The G major and E flat (' Emperor ') Concertos.

Third Period—Begins roughly with Op. 90.
    Pianoforte Sonata in E minor (Op. 90) *et seq.*
    Mass in D.
    Choral Symphony, No. 9 in D minor, Op. 125.
    String Quartets from Op. 127.

THE BEGINNING OF ROMANTICISM

SCHUBERT, Franz (1797-1828). Austrian. Born in Vienna.
Songs (603).
Song-cycles (3).
   ' The Lovely Maid of the Mill.'
   ' The Winter Journey.'
   ' Swan-songs.'
Choral Works.
   Masses (6).
   Cantatas.
     ' The Song of Miriam.'
Works for the Stage.
   ' Rosamunde.' (Incidental music.)
Chamber Music.
   Trios, Quartets, Quintets (' Trout ' Quintet), Octet.
Pianoforte Sonatas (24).
Symphonies (10).
   C major; B flat.
   ' Unfinished ' (B minor).

THE ROMANTIC COMPOSERS

WEBER, Carl Maria von (1786-1826). German. Opera composer
   ' Der Freischütz ' (The Marksman).
   ' Preciosa.' (Incidental music.)
   ' Euryanthe.'
   ' Oberon.' (Commissioned for the English stage.)

BERLIOZ, Hector (1803-1869). French. Born near Grenoble
Operas (3).
   ' Benvenuto Cellini.'
   ' Les Troyens ' (*The Trojans*).
   ' Beatrice e Benedict.'
Choral Works.
   ' Requiem ' (*Messe des Morts*).
   ' Te Deum.'
Symphonic Poems.
   ' Symphonie Fantastique ' (Episodes de la vie d'un artiste).
   ' Harold en Italie '—Symphony with solo viola.
   ' Romeo et Juliette '—Symphony for solo voices, chorus and
     orchestra.
Overtures (6) : ' King Lear ' ; ' Le Carnaval Romain.'
Book: an important treatise on ' Instrumentation'.

MENDELSSOHN-BARTHOLDY, Felix (1809-1847). German. Born at Hamburg.

Oratorios.
  ' St Paul.'
  ' Elijah.'

Symphony-Cantata.
  ' The Hymn of Praise ' (Lobgesang).

Overtures.
  ' A Midsummer Night's Dream.'
  ' Fingal's Cave.'
  ' Ruy Blas.'
  ' Calm Sea and Prosperous Voyage.'

Symphonies (5).
  ' Scotch ' (No. 3).
  ' Italian ' (No. 4).
  ' Reformation ' (No. 5).

Concerto.
  Violin Concerto in E minor.

Chamber Music.
  Pianoforte Trios, String Quartets, etc.

Pianoforte Music.
  ' Songs without Words.'   Prelude and Fugue in E minor.

Organ Sonatas (6).

SCHUMANN, Robert (1810-56). German. Born at Zwickau, Saxony.

Pianoforte Works.
  ' Abegg ' Variations (Op. 1).
  Toccata, Sonatas, Romances, etc.
  Sets of pieces ; ' Carnaval ' and ' Davidsbündler'.
  Pieces for pedal-piano.

Chamber Music.
  Pianoforte Trios, Quartets, Pianoforte Quintet, etc.

Choral Works (with Orchestra).
  ' Paradise and the Peri.'

Opera.
  ' Genoveva.'

Symphonies (4).

Songs.
  Song-cycle ' Dichterliebe ' (' The Poet's Love ').
  ' The Two Grenadiers,' etc.

CHOPIN, Frédéric (1810-49).   Polish.   Born near Warsaw.
Pianoforte Compositions.
  Ballades and Impromptus.
  Etudes.
  Mazurkas.
  Nocturnes.
  Polonaises.
  Preludes.
  Waltzes.
  Three Sonatas, two Pianoforte Concertos.
LISZT, Franz (1811-86).   Hungarian.   Born at Raiding.
Pianoforte Works.
  ' Années de Pélerinage.'
  Hungarian Rhapsodies.
  Etudes, etc.
  Arrangements and Transcriptions.
Orchestral Works.
  ' Faust ' Symphony.
  ' Dante ' Symphony.
  ' Orpheus ' and other Symphonic Poems.
Pianoforte Concertos (2).
Vocal Works.
  Masses, and an oratorio ' Christus'.
WAGNER, Richard (1813-83).   German.   Born at Leipzig.
Operas (12).
  ' Rienzi.'
  ' The Flying Dutchman.'
  ' Tannhäuser.'
  ' Lohengrin.'
  ' Tristan und Isolde.'
  ' Die Meistersinger.'
  ' The Ring '—a trilogy of music dramas with prologue :
      Das Rheingold (prologue), Die Walküre, Siegfried, and
      Götterdämmerung (Twilight of the Gods).
  ' Parsifal.'

VERDI, Giuseppe (1813-1901).   Italian.
Operas (31).
  (a) *Early*
      ' Nabucco ' ;   ' Ernani.'
  (b) *Middle period*
      ' Rigoletto ' ;   ' Il Trovatore ' ;   ' La Traviata ' ;   ' I vestri
        siciliani ' (' Sicilian Vespers ').
  (c) *Final period*
      ' Don Carlos ' ;   ' Aida ' ;   ' Otello ' ;   ' Falstaff.'
Choral Works.
  ' Requiem ' (in memory of Rossini).
Chamber Music.
  String Quartet in E minor.
FRANCK, César (1822-90).   Belgian.   Born at Liége.
  Symphony in D minor.
  Symphonic Poems : ' Les Djinns ' and ' Le Chasseur Maudit '.
  Symphonic Variations for Pianoforte and Orchestra.
Instrumental and Chamber Music.
  Prelude, Choral and Fugue for Pianoforte.
  Three Chorals for Organ.
  Sonata for Violin and Pianoforte.
  Pianoforte Quintet.
  String Quartet.
Choral Music.
  ' The Beatitudes.'
  ' The Redemption.'
BRAHMS, Johannes (1833-1897).   German.   Born at Hamburg.
Symphonies (4).
  No. 1 in C minor, No. 2 in D, No. 3 in F, No. 4 in E minor.
Overtures.
  The ' Tragic'.
  The ' Academic Festival '.
Concertos.
  Pianoforte, Violin, Violin and Violoncello.
Pianoforte Sonatas (3).

Variations for Pianoforte.
   —on a theme by Paganini.
   —on a theme by Schumann.
   —on a theme by Handel.
Songs (230).
Vocal Works.
   ' The German Requiem.'
   ' The Song of Destiny.'
   ' The Song of Triumph.'
Chamber Music.
   Pianoforte Trios, Quartets, and Quintet.   String Quartets
      Quintets, and Sextets.   Quintet for Clarinet and Strings, etc

NATIONALISTS

TCHAIKOVSKY, Peter Ilich (1840-1893).   Russian.
Symphonies (6).
   No. 4 in F minor ;   No. 5 in E minor.
   No. 6 (' The Pathetique ') in B minor.
Concertos (4).
   Pianoforte Concerto No. 1 in B♭ minor.
Overtures.
   ' Romeo and Juliet.'
   ' 1812.'
Symphonic Poem.
   ' Francesca da Rimini.'
Orchestral Suite.
   ' Casse Noisette ' (*Nutcracker Suite*).
Chamber Music.
   String Quartets (3).
   Pianoforte Trio in A minor.
Operas and Ballets.
   ' Eugen Onegin ' (Opera).
   ' Swan Lake ' (Ballet).
   ' The Sleeping Beauty ' (Ballet).
Songs.   (Over 100.)

DVORAK (1841-1904). Bohemian. Born at Mühlhausen.
Orchestral Works.
Symphonies (9) : No. 2 in D min., No. 4 in G, No. 5 in E min.
('New World').
'Three Slavonic Dances.'
'Symphonic Variations on an Original Theme.'
Choral Works.
'The Spectre's Bride'. (Cantata).
'Stabat Mater.'
Chamber Music.
Pianoforte Trios ('Dumky' Trio) ; String Quartets ('Nigger
Quartet'); Pianoforte Quartet and Quintet; String
'Terzetto' and 'Bagatelles'.
Songs—upwards of 100 including the 'Ten Biblical Songs'.
GRIEG, Edvard (1843-1907). Norwegian.
Orchestral Works.
'Peer Gynt' Suites 1 and 2 (Incidental Music to Ibsen's play).
'Holberg Suite' (arranged for String orchestra).
Pianoforte Concerto in A minor.
Chamber Music.
Sonatas : Pianoforte (1) ; Violin and Pianoforte (3) ; 'Cello
and Pianoforte (1) ; String Quartet.
Pianoforte Music. 'Poetic Tone-pictures'; 'Humoresques'.
Songs (130).
PUCCINI, Giacomo (1858-1924). Italian.
Operas (12).
'La Boheme.'
'Tosca.'
'Madam Butterfly.'
'Turandot.'
Church music ; choral and orchestral works ; chamber music
and songs.

LATE ROMANTICS

STRAUSS, Richard (1864-1949). German. Born in Munich.
Operas (15).
'Salome.'
'Elektra.'
'Der Rosenkavalier' (*Knight of the Rose*).

Symphonic Poems.
  ' Don Juan.'
  ' Death and Transfiguration.'
  ' Till Eulenspiegel ' (' Till Owlglass's Merry Tricks ').
  ' Don Quixote '—Fantasy variations.
  ' A Hero's Life.'
  ' A Domestic Symphony.'
Songs (over 120).
ELGAR, Edward (1857-1934). British. Born at Worcester.
Oratorios.
  ' The Dream of Gerontius.'
  ' The Apostles.'
  ' The Kingdom.'
Orchestral Works.
  The ' Enigma ' Variations.
  Concert Overture : ' Cockaigne '.
  Symphonic Poem : ' Falstaff '.
  Two Symphonies : No. 1 in A flat, No. 2 in E flat.
Concertos.
  For Violin, and for Violoncello.
Chamber Music.
  String Quartet.
  Piano Quintet.
                    THE TWENTIETH CENTURY
DEBUSSY, Claude (1862-1918).   French.
Orchestral Pieces.
  ' Afternoon of a Faun ' (L'après-midi d'un faune).
  Three Nocturnes.
  ' The Sea ' (La Mer)—symphonic sketches.
Opera.
  ' Pelléas et Mélisande.'
Pianoforte Pieces.
  ' La Cathédrale Engloutie.'
  ' Gardens in the Rain.'
  ' Reflections in the Water.'
  ' Children's Corner ' Suite, etc.

Chamber Music.
  String Quartet in G minor.
  Sonatas (3) for 'Cello and Pianoforte ; Violin and Pianoforte,
    and for Flute, Viola and Harp.
Songs (50).
RAVEL, Maurice (1875-1937).   French.
Orchestral Music.
  ' Rhapsodie Espagnole.'
  ' Le Tombeau de Couperin.'
  ' Bolero.'
Operas (2).
  ' L'Heure Espagnole.'
  ' L'Enfant et les Sortilèges.'
Ballets for Orchestra.
  ' Daphnis et Chloë.'
  ' Ma Mère l'Oye (also as Pianoforte duet).
Chamber Music.
  String Quartet in F.
  Piano Trio.
  Sonatas for Violin and Pianoforte (2).
Pianoforte Solo.
  Sonatina ; ' Jeux d'eau ' ; ' Miroirs ' ; ' Le Tombeau de
    Couperin '.
Songs (30).
DELIUS, Frederick (1862-1934).   Born at Bradford.   Parents
  naturalized British.
Orchestral Works.
  ' Paris ' (Nocturne).
  ' On hearing the first Cuckoo in Spring.'
  ' Brigg Fair.'
  ' Dance Rhapsody ' (1 and 2).
Concertos : Pianoforte ; Violin ; 'Cello.
Operas (6).
  ' Koanga.'
  ' A Village Romeo and Juliet.'
Choral-Orchestra Works (8).
  ' Sea Drift.'
  ' A Mass of Life.'

Chamber Music : Sonatas for Violin and Pianoforte (3).
'Cello and Pianoforte (1).

Songs (43) ; Song Cycle, and Pianoforte Pieces.

NIELSEN, Carl (1865-1931). Danish.

Operas, Stage Works and Incidental Music.

Choral Works.

    Cantatas (10) ; Motets, etc.

Orchestral Works.

    ' Little Suite ' for Strings.

    Overtures : ' Helius ' and ' Rhapsodic Overture '.

    Symphonies (6).

Concertos : Violin.

             Flute.

             Clarinet.

Chamber Music.

    String Quartets (4).

    Quintet for Wind Instruments.

    Sonatas for Violin and Pianoforte.

    Pieces for Oboe and Pianoforte ; Clarinet and Pianoforte ; Solo Pianoforte and Organ.

Songs.

SIBELIUS, Jean (1865-1957). Finnish.

Orchestral Works.

    Symphonies (7) (8th unfinished).

    Overtures : ' Karelia '.

    Tone-poems : ' En Saga ' ; ' Finlandia '.

    Legend : ' The Swan of Tuonela '.

    Symphonic Poems : ' Tapiola ' ; ' The Oceanides '.

Choral Works—with orchestra, with organ, and unaccompanied.

Solo Instrument with Orchestra.

    Violin Concerto in D minor.

Chamber Music.

    String Quartet in D minor (' Voces Intimae ').

    Sonatas for Violin and Pianoforte.

             'Cello and Pianoforte.

    Numerous pieces for Pianoforte Solo.

Songs (about 90) and a Song Cycle.

VAUGHAN WILLIAMS, Ralph (1872-1958). English. Born in Gloucestershire.

Symphonies (9).
'A Sea Symphony' (Chorus and Orchestra).
'A London Symphony.'
'Pastoral Symphony.'
Symphony No. 4 in F minor ; No. 5 in D ; No. 6 in E minor ; No. 7 in D minor (*Sinfonia Antarctica*) ; No. 8 in D minor ; No. 9 in E minor.

Orchestral Works.
'The Wasps' (Incidental music to Aristophanes' Comedy).
'Five Variants on *Dives and Lazarus.*'
'Fantasy on a Theme by Tallis.'
'Concerto Grosso for Strings.'

Solo Instruments and Orchestra.
'The Lark Ascending' (Violin and Orchestra).
'Concerto Accademica' (Violin and Strings).
'Suite for Viola.'
Concertos : Oboe and Strings ; Two Pianofortes.

Choral Works.
'Towards the Unknown Region.'
'Five Mystical Songs' (Baritone, chorus and orchestra).
'Sancta Civitas' (oratorio).
'Benedicite.'
'Dona Nobis Pacem.'
'Five Tudor Portraits.'
'Flos Campi' (Suite for Viola, chorus and orchestra).
'The Pilgrim's Progress' (oratorio).
'Hodie.'

Chamber Music.
String Quartet.
Preludes on Welsh Hymn tunes ('Household Music') for Strings.

Song Cycles.
'On Wenlock Edge' (Housman).

Songs and Folk-songs (with Pianoforte accompaniment).

Books : 'National Music', etc.

IRELAND, John (1879-1962). English.
Orchestral Works.
    Prelude : ' The Forgotten Rite.'
    Symphonic Rhapsody : ' Mai-Dun.'
    ' A London Overture.'
    ' Epic March.'
    ' Concertino Pastorale ' for String Orchestra.
Concerto for Pianoforte (E flat).
Chamber Music.
    Pianoforte Trios (3).
    Sonata and Sonatina for Pianoforte.
    Sonatas for Violin and Pianoforte (2).
    ' Phantasy-Sonata ' for Clarinet and Pianoforte.
Choral Works.
    Motet : ' Greater Love hath No Man ' (choir, orchestra and
       organ).
    Morning and Evening Services.
    ' These Things Shall Be ' (choir and orchestra).
Pianoforte Pieces.
    Preludes ; ' London Pieces', etc.

Songs and Song Cycles.
    Songs : ' Sea Fever ' ; Hardy Songs, etc.
    Song Cycles : ' Songs of a Wayfarer ' (Rossetti).
                    ' The Land of Lost Content ' (Housman).
BAX, Sir Arnold (1883-1953). English. Master of the Queen's
    Music.
Orchestral Works.
    Symphonies (7).
    ' Overture to a Picaresque Comedy.'
    Symphonic Poems : ' November Woods.'
                    ' The Garden of Fand.'
                    ' Tintagel.'
    Symphonic Variations for Pianoforte and Orchestra.
    Concertos : Violin ; 'Cello.
Choral Music.
    ' Enchanted Summer.'
    ' Mater Ora Filium ' and other unaccompanied motets.

Chamber Music.
   Harp Trio ; Quintet for Harp and Strings.
   String Quartets ; Pianoforte Quartet and Quintet.
   Sonatas for Violin and Pianoforte (3) ; Viola and Pianoforte ;
      'Cello.
   Pianoforte Sonatas (4) and Sonata for Two Pianofortes.
Songs and Folk-song arrangements.
SCHOENBERG, Arnold (1874-1951).   Austrian.
Operas (4).
   ' Moses and Aaron.'
Orchestral Works (4).
   ' Pelléas und Melisande.'   (Symphonic Poem.)
   ' Five Pieces.'
Choral Works (12).
   ' Gurrelieder ' (Songs of Gurra) with orchestra.
   ' Friede auf Erden ' (Unaccompanied chorus).
Voice with Orchestra.
   Songs (10).
Sprechstimme (Half-reciting with orchestra) :
   ' Pierrot Lunaire '—Cycle of 21 songs.
Songs with Pianoforte (8 Sets).
Chamber Music.
   String Quartets (4) ; String Sextet : ' Verklärte Nacht '.
   ' Chamber Symphony ' for 15 solo instruments.
Pianoforte Music.
   ' Three Pieces ' ; ' Suite ', and ' Klavierstück.'
Treatises : on Harmony ; Composition : Counterpoint.
STRAVINSKY, Igor (1882-1971). Russian.
Ballet Music for Orchestra.
   ' The Fire Bird ' (*L'oiseau de Feu*).
   ' Petrouchka.'
   ' The Rite of Spring.'
Operas.
   ' The Rake's Progress.'
Choral-Orchestral Works.
   ' Oedipus Rex ' (Opera-oratorio).
   ' Symphony of Psalms.'

Orchestral Works.
   ' Fireworks.'
   ' Symphony for Wind Instruments.'
   Symphonies for full Orchestra (3).
Concertos : Pianoforte (2) ; for Two Pianofortes (1) ; for Violin (1).
Chamber Music.
   ' Octet for Wind Instruments.'
Sonatas for Pianoforte (2) ; for two pianofortes (1). Piano pieces exemplifying ' serial ' technique.
Songs (17).
BARTÓK, Béla (1881-1945).   Hungarian.
Operas and Mime-plays.
   ' Bluebeard's Castle ' (opera).
   ' The Wooden Prince ' (mime-play).
Orchestral Works.
   ' Two Portraits.'
   ' Two Pictures.'
   ' Dance Suites (2).
   ' Music for Strings, Percussion and Celesta.
   ' Concerto for Orchestra.'
Solo Instruments and Orchestra.
   Concertos : Pianoforte (3) ; Violin ; Viola.
   Rhapsodies for Violin and Orchestra (2).
   Rhapsody for Pianoforte and Orchestra.
Choral Music.
   ' Cantata Profana ' for solo voices, choir and orchestra.
Chamber Music.
   String Quartets (6) : Violin and Pianoforte Sonatas (2).
   Pianoforte Sonata and Sonatina.
   Sonata for Unaccompanied Violin.
Pianoforte Music.
   ' Mikrokosmos ' (153 progressive pieces).
   ' Bagatelles for Children.'
   ' Burlesques ' ; ' Rumanian Dances.'
Songs—Extensive collections, and many arrangements of Hungarian, Slovak and Rumanian folk-songs.

WEBERN, Anton (von) (1883-1945).   Austrian.
Orchestral Works.
 ' Passacaglia ' (Op. 1) for full orchestra.
 ' Symphony ' (Op. 21) for clarinets, horns, harp and strings.
 ' Variations ' for small orchestra including tuba.
Choral Works.
 ' Das Augenlicht ' (*Vision*) (Chorus and Orchestra).
 Cantatas (2) for solo voice(s), chorus and orchestra.
Chamber Music.
 ' Five Movements ' for string quartet.
 ' Six Bagatelles ' for string quartet.
 String Trio (Violin, viola and 'cello).
Five Canons for voice, clarinet and bass clarinet.
Pianoforte Solo.
 ' Variations.'
Pieces for : Violin and Pianoforte (4).
              'Cello and Pianoforte (3).
Songs (20).
BERG, Alban (1885-1935). Austrian. .
Operas.
 ' Wozzeck.'
 ' Lulu.'
Works with Orchestra.
 Concerto for Violin and Orchestra (' To the Memory of an
    Angel ').
 ' Five Songs ' (Picture-postcard texts).
 ' Der Wein '—Concert aria for soprano (3 poems by Baude-
    laire).
Chamber Music.
 ' Chamber Concerto ' for Pianoforte, Violin and 13 Wind
    instruments.
 ' Lyric Suite ' for String Quartet.
Pianoforte Solo.
 Sonata, Op. 1.
Songs (14).

PROKOFIEV, Sergey Sergéyvitch (1891-1953). Russian

Operas.
' The Love of Three Oranges.'
' War and Peace.'

Ballets.
' Romeo and Juliet.'
' Cinderella.'

Orchestral Works.
Symphonies (6).
' A Scythian Suite.'
' Classical Symphony ' (Reflection of Mozart).
' Russian ' Overture.
' Egyptian Night ' (Suite—Incidental music to Shakespeare and Shaw).

Concertos : Pianoforte (4)—one for left hand.
Violin (2) ; 'Cello (1).

Chamber Music.
String Quartets : Quintet for Wind and Pianoforte.
' Overture ' on Hebrew themes (Clarinet, strings and piano-forte).
Sonatas : Violin and Pianoforte ; 'Cello and Pianoforte.
Pianofort: Sonatas (8).

Choral Work.
' Seven. They are Seven ' for tenor, choir and orchestra.

Songs and numerous pieces for Pianoforte.

HONEGGER, Arthur (1892-1955). Swiss.

Operas.
' Antigone ' (after Sophocles).
' Judith.'

Ballets.
' Sailor Bar ' ; ' The Skating Rink '.

Oratorios.
' King David ' (Biblical Opera).
' Jeanne d'Arc au bucher ' (Oratorio).

Orchestral Works.
    ' Symphony ' ;   Symphony for Strings (' Spring 1946 in Prague ').
    Symphonic Movements : ' Pacific ' ; ' Rugby '.
    Mimed Symphony (' Horace Victorieux ').
Concertos : 'Cello and Orchestra.
            Pianoforte and Orchestra (Concertino).
Chamber Music.
    String Quartet.
    Sonatas : 'Violin and Pianoforte (2).
            'Cello and Pianoforte ; Viola and Pianoforte.
    Sonatinas for two violins and for clarinet.
    ' Chansons ' for voice, flute and string quartet.
Songs, pianoforte compositions and organ pieces.
HINDEMITH, Paul (1895-1963). German.
Operas (7).
    ' Mathis de Maler ' (*Mathias the Painter*).
Orchestral Works.
    ' Nobilissima Visione ' (ballet).
    ' Symphony based on material of ' Mathis der Maler.'
    Symphony in E flat.
    ' Symphonic Metamorphoses on a Theme by Weber.'
Choral Music.
    ' The Undefinable ' (*Das Unaufhorliche*)—Oratorio for chorus, boys' choir and orchestra.
Concertos.
    Viola and Small Orchestra (' Der Schwanendreher'—*The Herder of Swans*).
    Violin and Orchestra (1939) ; 'Cello and Orchestra ; Organ and Chamber Orchestra ; Pianoforte Concerto ; Horn Concerto.
Chamber Music.
    Piano Trio ; String Trio ; String Quartets (7) ; Wind Quintet ; ' Kammermusik ' (Nos. 2-3)—Concertos for Pianoforte, 'Cello, and 12 and 10 solo instruments, respectively.
    Sonatas for Wind instruments with Pianoforte (8).

Pianoforte Music.

    Sonatas (3) ; Sonata for Two Pianofortes.

    ' Ludus Tonalis ' (' Tonal Game ' in form of Preludes and Fugues).

Songs and Song-Cycles.

    ' Das Marienleben ' (Rilke Cycle).

    ' Chansons ' for Unaccompanied Choir.

' *Gebrauchsmusik* ' (Music for practical purposes).

    ' Let Us build a City ' (Cantata for Schools).

    ' Music for 2 Male voices, narrator, choir, orchestra, dancer, clown and community singing,' and many other works.

COPLAND, Aaron (b. 1900, Brooklyn N.Y.).   American.

Ballets, Film and Incidental Music.

    ' Billy the Kid.' (Ballet).

    ' Appalachian Spring ' (Ballet).

Orchestral Works.

    ' A Dance Symphony ' (exemplifying jazz techniques).

    ' El Salon Mexico.'

    Symphonies (3) and ' Symphonic Ode '.

    Symphony for Organ and Orchestra.

Concertos : Piano and Orchestra.

             Clarinet and Orchestra.

Speaker and Orchestra.

    ' Lincoln Portrait.'

Chamber Music.

    ' Vitebsk ' (Piano trio).

    String Quartet.

    Sextet for Clarinet, string quartet and pianoforte.

    Sonata for Violin and Pianoforte.

Pianoforte : Sonata.

           ' Passacaglia.'

           ' Four Piano Blues.'

           ' Danzan Cuban ' for *two* pianofortes.

WALTON, Sir William (b. 1902 at Oldham).   English.
Opera.
  ' Troilus and Cressida.'
Orchestral Works.
  Symphony No. 1 in B flat minor.
  Symphony No. 2.
  Overtures : ' Portsmouth Point '.
              ' Scapino ' (Comedy Overture).
              ' Johannesburg Festival Overture '.
  Marches : ' Crown Imperial ' ; ' Orb and Sceptre '.
Speaker and Small Ensemble.
  ' Facade ' Suites, Nos. I and II.
Choral-Orchestral Works.
  ' Belshazzer's Feast.'
  ' In Honour of the City of London.'
Concertos.
  ' Sinfonia concertante ', for orchestra with pianoforte.
  Violin Concerto ; Viola Concerto ; 'Cello Concerto.
Chamber Music.
  String Quartets (2) ; Sonata for Violin and Pianoforte.
Songs : ' Bucolic Comedies ' ; ' Three Songs ', etc.
SHOSTAKOVICH, Dimitri (b. 1906). Russian.   . .
Operas, Ballets and incidental music to plays including Shakes-
  peare's ' Hamlet ', ' King Lear ' and ' Othello '.
Film music.
Symphonies (11). No. 7 : ' Leningrad Symphony '.
Concerto for Piano, Trumpet and Strings.
Chamber Music. String Quartets (2) ; String Octet music ;
  Piano Trio and Piano Quintet.
  Sonata for 'Cello and Piano.
Pianoforte sonatas ; 24 Preludes and Fugues and numerous
  piano pieces.
Songs: 4 Romances to poems by Pushkin.
  Song Cycle on Japanese poems.
New Orchestration of Mussorgsky's opera ' Boris Godunov '.

BRITTEN, Benjamin (b. 1913 at Lowestoft). English.
Operas (7).
　'Peter Grimes.'
　'The Rape of Lucretia.'
　'Albert Herring.'
　'Let's Make an Opera.'
　'The Turn of the Screw.'
　'Billy Budd.'
Choral Works.
　'A Boy was Born' (Choral Variations).
　'A Ceremony of Carols' (Treble voices and Harp).
　'Spring Symphony' (Solo voice, chorus and orchestra).
　'Rejoice in the Lamb' (Festival Cantata).
Orchestral Works.
　'Sinfonietta' for Chamber Orchestra.
　'Variations on a Theme by Frank Bridge (String Orchestra).
　'Sinfonia da Requiem' (in memory of his parents).
　'The Young Person's Guide to the Orchestra' (Variations on
　　a theme by Purcell).
Concertos.
　Pianoforte and Orchestra.
　Violin and Orchestra.
　'Diversions on a Theme' (Pianoforte (left hand) and orches-
　　tra).
Chamber Music.
　'Fantasy Quartet' (Oboe and strings).
　String Quartets (2).
Song Cycles, Songs and Folk-song arrangements.
　'Les Illuminations' (Soprano or Tenor and String Orchestra).
　'Seven Sonnets of Michelangelo' for Tenor and Pianoforte.
　'Serenade' for Tenor, Horn and String Orchestra.
　'A Charm of Lullabies'; 'Winter Words'.

COMPARATIVE CHRONOLOGY

English Writers	Painters and Sculptors	Composers
...ucer (1340?-1400)	Giotto (1276-1336). It. Van Eyck (1385-1441). Flem. *Donatello* (1386-1466). It. Fra Angelico (1387-1455). It. Masaccio (1401-1428). Flor.	JOHN DUNSTABLE (1390-1453). Eng.
...ory, Sir Thomas (d. 1471) ...e, Sir Thomas (1478-1535)	Piero della Francesca (1410/20-92). Flor. Bellini (1426-1516). It. Botticelli (1444-1510). It. Leonardo da Vinci (1452-1519). It. Dürer (1471-1528). Ger. *Michelangelo* (1475-1564). It. Raphael (1483-1520?). It. Titian (c. 1487/90-1576). (Ven.) Holbein (1497-1543). Ger.	JOSQUIN DES PRES (1445-1521). Flem.
...nser, Edmund (1552-1599) ...owe, Christopher (1564-...93) ...kespeare (1564-1616) ...son, Ben (1573?-1637)	El Greco (1547-1614). Sp. Brueghel (1525/30-1569). Flem. Rubens (1577-1640). Flem. Poussin (1594-1665). Fr. *Bernini* (1598-1680). It. Vandyck (1599-1641). Flem. Velasquez (1599-1660). Sp.	PALESTRINA (1526-1594). It. WILLIAM BYRD (1543-1623). Eng. THOMAS MORLEY (1557-1603?). Eng. MONTEVERDI (1567-1643). It.
...on (1608-1674) ...yan (1628-1688) ...ien (1631-1700) ...t (1667-1745) ...e (1688-1744) ...ding, Henry (1707-1754) ...son, Samuel (1709-1784) ...y (1716-1771) ...idan (1751-1816) ...e (1759-1827) ...dsworth (1770-1850) ...t (1771-1832) ...en, Jane (1775-1817) ...s (1791-1821) ...ey (1792-1822)	Rembrandt (1606-1669). Dutch Vermeer (1632-1675). Dutch Watteau (1684-1721). Fr. Hogarth (1697-1764). Brit. Chardin (1699-1779). Fr. Wilson (1713-1782). Brit. Reynolds (1723-1792). Brit. Gainsborough (1727-1788). Brit. Goya (1746-1828). Sp. David Jacques (1748-1825). Fr. Turner (1775-1851). Brit. Constable (1776-1837). Brit. Ingres (1780-1867). Fr.	PURCELL (1658/9-1695). Eng. BACH, J. S. (1685-1750). Ger. HANDEL (1685-1759). Ger. GLUCK (1714-1787). Ger. HAYDN (1732-1809). Aust. MOZART (1756-1791). Aust. BEETHOVEN (1770-1827). Ger. WEBER (1786-1826). Ger. SCHUBERT (1797-1828). Aust.
...yson (1809-1892) ...ens (1812-1870) ...ning (1812-1889)	Corot (1796-1875). Fr. Delacroix (1798-1863). Fr. Courbet (1819-1877). Fr.	BERLIOZ (1803-1869). Fr. GLINKA (1804-1857). Russ. MENDELSSOHN (1809-1847). Ger. CHOPIN (1810-1849). Pol. SCHUMANN (1810-1856). Ger.

English Writers	Painters and Sculptors	Composers
Brontë, Emily (1814-48) Charlotte (1816-55)	Millais (1829-1896). Br.	LISZT (1811-1886). Hung. WAGNER (1813-1883). Ger.
	Manet (1832-1883). Fr.	VERDI (1813-1901). It.
Rossetti, Christina (1830-1894)	Whistler (1834-1903). Am.	FRANCK (1822-1890). Belgia
	Degas (1834-1917). Fr.	BRAHMS (1833-1897). Ger.
Swinburne (1837-1909)	Cezanne (1839-1906). Fr.	BORODIN (1834-1887). Russ.
	Rodin (1840-1917). Fr.	MOUSSORGSKY (1839-1881). I
Hardy, Thomas (1840-1928)	Monet (1840-1926)	TCHAIKOVSKY (1840-1893). I
Bridges, Robert (1844-1930)	Renoir (1841-1919). Fr.	DVORAK (1841-1904). Boh.
Stevenson, Robert Louis	Gaugin (1849-1903). Fr.	GRIEG (1843-1907). Norwegi
(1850-1894).	Van Gogh (1853-1890). Dutch	RIMSKY-KORSAKOV (1844-1
	Maillol (1861-1944). Fr.	Russ.
Shaw, George Bernard (1856-1950)		PUCCINI (1858/9-24). It. ELGAR (1857-1934). Br. DEBUSSY (1862-1918). Fr. RAVEL (1875-1937). Fr.
Kipling, Rudyard (1865-1936)		DELIUS (1863-1934). Brit.
Yeats, W. B. (1865-1939)	Matisse (1869-1954). Fr.	STRAUSS (1864-1949). Ger.
Galsworth, John (1867-1933)	Mondrian (1872-1944). Dutch	NIELSEN (1865-1931). Danis
Wells, H. G. (1866-1946)		SIBELIUS (b. 1865-1957). Fir VAUGHAN WILLIAMS (1872-1 Br.
		HOLST (1874-1934). Brit.
	Brancusi (1876-1957). Roumanian.	SCHOENBERG (1874-1951). A IRELAND, JOHN (1879-1962
Masefield, John (1878-1967)	Paul Klee (1879-1940). Swiss John, Augustus (1878-1961). Brit.	PIZZETTI (1880-1968). It. BARTOK (1881-1945). Hun
Forster, E. M. (1879-1972)		STRAVINSKY (1882-1971). I
Joyce, James (1882-1941)	*Epstein* (1880-1959). Br.	BAX (1883-1953). Brit.
Lawrence, D. H. (1885-1930)	Picasso (1881-1973). Sp.	WEBERN (1883-1945). Aust.
de la Mare, Walter (1873-1956)	Paul Nash (1889-1946). Brit.	BERG (1885-1935). Aust.
Eliot, T. S. (1888-1965)		PROKOFIEV (1891-1953). Rus BLISS, SIR ARTHUR (b. 1891
	Moore, Henry (b. 1898). Brit.	HONEGGER (1892-1955). Swi HINDEMITH (1895-1963). C HARRIS, ROY (b. 1898). Am. COPLAND, AARON (b. 1900). RUBBRA, EDMUND (b. 1901).
	Hepworth, Barbara (b. 1903) Brit.	WALTON, WILLIAM (b. 1902). Brit.
Day Lewis, Cecil (1904-1973)		SHOSTAKOVITCH (b. 1906). R
Auden, W. H. (1907-1974)		BERKELEY, LENNOX (b. 1 Brit. TIPPETT, MICHAEL (b. 1905). RAWSTHORNE, ALAN (1905- Brit. LUTYENS, ELISABETH (b. 1 Brit.
Thomas, Dylan (1914-1953)		BRITTEN, BENJAMIN (b. 1 Brit. SEARLE, HUMPHREY (b. 1 Brit. SIBELIUS (1865-1959). Fin.

KEY—Am. = American. Aust. = Austrian. Bav. = Bavarian. Boh. = Bohemian. Brit. = B
Dan. = Danish. Eng. = English. Finn. = Finnish. Flem. = Flemish. Flor. = Florentine. Fr. = Fr
Ger. = German. Hung. = Hungarian. It. = Italian. Pol. = Polish. Russ. = Russian. Sp. = Spa
Sw. = Swiss. Ven. = Venetian

INDEX

251